On Becoming Birthwise

Books in this Series

ON BECOMING

BIRTH WISE

Anne Marie Ezzo, R.N.; Sharon Nelson, M.D.;
Diane Dirks, C.N.M.; Pam Harer, R.N.;
Sharon Augustson, R.N.; Kathy Hoefke, R.N.

ON BECOMING BIRTHWISE

Birth by Design

Published by Parent-Wise Solutions, Inc.

(A Division of the Charleston Publishing Group, Inc.)

© 2003 by Anne Marie Ezzo, R.N.; Sharon Nelson, M.D.; Diane Dirks, C.N.M.;
Pam Harer, R.N.; Sharon Augustson, R.N.; Kathy Hoefke, R.N.

International Standard Book Number:

0-9714532-6-8

Printed in the United States of America

For more information:

Parent-Wise Solutions, Inc.

2130 Cheswick Lane,

Mt. Pleasant, South Carolina 29466

04 05 06 07 – 7 6 5 4 3 2

Dedication:

To the encouragers of our lives – our husbands and children – and to those parents who seek to know how to raise their children wisely.

ACKNOWLEDGMENTS

The authors wish to express sincere gratitude to all those who helped by providing information, those who spent hours inputting data and editing, and especially our friends and families, who faithfully supported us throughout this project.

CONTENTS

USING THIS BOOK

The material in *On Becoming Birthwise* is meant to be used in conjunction with ongoing care from a health-care provider. Ultimately, prospective parents are responsible for making decisions about the birth experience, and it is important for them to consult their health-care provider with all their concerns. Because each individual case is unique, there will be variations in the application of the general principles presented here.

FOREWORD

There is no shortage of books on childbirth. While casually browsing at my local bookstore, I saw more than fifty-feet of shelf space devoted to the topic. The variety of books offered is amazing. There are books by doctors, nurses, midwives—and just about everybody else with an opinion!

According to an old proverb, "There is only one way to be born, but a thousand ways to die." These days, though, there are many ways to be born. From conception to delivery, there are endless choices with more options becoming available every day. Medical research continually comes up with better ways to do things and with new answers to problems. With all of the choices available, it is a growing challenge for expectant parents to make all the decisions necessary to take them through the process of pregnancy, labor, and delivery.

Looking over the sea of books available, I am delighted to see *On Becoming Birthwise*. An outgrowth of a childbirth course created by a group of health-care providers experienced in childbirth education, the material in this book has been used by thousands of expectant parents with great success since 1989. Like the subsequent books in the *"On Becoming"* series, it will give you the plain talk and practical help you need to make decisions with confidence as your family grows. It will answer your questions, describe the medical options available, explain the risks and benefits of all the common procedures and practices, and tell you what to expect from medical providers and how to work with them.

I am happy to recommend *On Becoming Birthwise* to expectant parents everywhere. Here you will find the medical information you need to make wise choices and move confidently through the process of pregnancy and birth.

D. C. Frame, M.D.

A New Life

*B*earing down with tremendous effort, she works at pushing the waiting life out of her body. Her husband wipes her beaded brow and gives her a supportive word, and she continues her courageous work.

Finally, a hairy scalp emerges. Forehead, eyes, nose, mouth, and chin follow, and the parents get their first glimpse of the little person they have dreamed about for months. With blinking eyes and puckered lips, the passenger completes the journey. As the baby slides into the waiting hands of the birth attendant, a new citizen is announced.

It's a girl!

The baby's first breath is the culmination of a perfectly timed, physiologically detailed plan. For nine months she has depended on her mother for survival, as the intricate workings of the placenta sustained her life. Now changes occur to ensure her independent survival. For the first time her heart pumps blood into her lungs, and the designated vessels close to complete the self-contained breathing process. With that first breath, she's on her own.

As the birth attendant cuts the umbilical cord, the parents celebrate their baby's first step of independence and the part they have played in the amazing process of birth that has design.

INTRODUCTION

In *The Seven Laws of the Learner*, Bruce Wilkinson writes that "every message has an irreducible minimum"—a kernel of important truth that will stand out even if no other information is remembered.[1] The most important kernel of truth in this book is the human ability to examine, evaluate, and choose with confidence birthing options available today.

Pregnancy and childbirth require us to make many important decisions, and to make wise ones, we must prepare our minds as well as our bodies. Becoming *"birthwise"* means learning to distinguish between what is "in" and what is best for us. Why is this important? Because culture isn't static. It changes over time in response to social, environmental, and technological changes, and as it does, birthing practices also change.[2]

In *On Becoming Birthwise*, our goal is to give you reliable information about every aspect of childbirth and increase your understanding of the amazing changes that take place in your body. We explain the role medical procedures play, discuss the options available, and encourage in-depth, open communication between you and your health-care providers, all in the hope of promoting healthy outcomes.

We know the information shared in this book will help prepare you not only for labor and the birth of your child, but also help set you on the right course for a lifetime relationship with that child.

Chapter One

Is It Time?

Seventeen-year-old Josh dreamed of flying airplanes. One day his father, Jim, a licensed pilot, invited him to take a short flight in his single-engine four-passenger airplane. Once the plane was in the air, Jim asked Josh if he would like to take the controls. Would he! It was like a dream come true. His father gave him a few instructions, and trying to ignore the butterflies in his stomach, Josh took over the controls. Flying was even more fun than he had imagined—until he attempted a diving roll. After that maneuver, he couldn't see anything but blue sky. Where was the ground? At first Jim let him try to figure things out on his own, but after about one minute of sheer terror, the experienced pilot took control of the plane.

Josh's experience pictures what it is like to feel totally inadequate when facing a potential life-and-death situation. While few of us will find ourselves in a plane looking for terra firma, many of us will have to make choices about pregnancy and childbirth that have life-and-death implications.

Of course, making a decision to have a baby is no more danger-ous than making a decision to fly a plane and neither has the poten-tial of danger until the first step is realized. For a pilot, it is stepping into the cockpit and turning on the engines. For a couple, it is actually conceiving a child that in nine months will go through a birthing process. While both starts have hopeful and reasonably predictable outcomes, both starts can also lead to the potential of life-or-death consequences.

Making A Timely Decision

One of the most important decisions prospective parents must make is if, and when to try to conceive. You must decide whether you are ready to add a child to your family. If you're not, you'll need to think about ways to try to prevent conception. In Appendix B, "Conception Prevention," we describe the kinds of contraceptives available, how they work, and their advantages and disadvantages.[3]

What to Do Before You Try to Conceive

Stop Using Contraceptives

This is fairly obvious. If you've been on oral contraceptives, you'll need to be off them for about a month before you try to conceive. They leave your body quickly, so even if conception occurs the first month, there is no increase in the risk of birth defects. If you had a history of irregular menstrual cycles before you began using oral contraceptives, you might want to be off them for several months before you try to conceive. Ovulation is unpredictable during the first month, and knowing the approximate time of ovulation helps your doctor determine your due-date.

See Your Doctor

Let your doctor know that you're planning to get pregnant, and get a complete physical exam, including a Pap smear. Your doctor will ask if you've ever had gynecological problems such as irregular cycles or infections or medical conditions such as Diabetes, Hypertension, or Epilepsy. If you're diabetic, you'll need to see your doctor several months before trying to conceive to make sure your diabetes is under control.

Have any Necessary Tests

If you aren't sure if you've been immunized for rubella, you'll need a blood test to find out. If you're not immune, you should be vaccinated three months before you try to conceive. Your doctor may recommend other blood tests to screen for Diabetes, Anemia, HIV, and sexually-transmitted diseases (STDs).

Find out if there is a history of genetic diseases or birth defects in your family. If there is, your doctor may refer you to a genetic counselor for an in-depth review of your history and possible carrier testing.

Review Your Habits

Your doctor will ask if you smoke or drink. If you smoke, you absolutely must quit before you try to conceive. If your husband smokes, he should quit too, but if he continues, make sure he does it away from you. Your doctor will also want to know if you use recreational drugs and if you've been exposed to toxic chemicals or pesticides. You should let him know about any medications and herbal products you're taking.

Your diet is important during pregnancy and needs to be reviewed. Obesity is associated with Diabetes and Hypertension, which can increase the risk of problems during pregnancy. Let your doctor know if you've had eating disorders such as bulimia or anorexia. If you're a vegetarian, you may want to consult a nutritionist to make sure you're getting enough protein. You'll also need to review your current exercise program, as you may have to modify it during pregnancy.

Start Taking a Multivitamin

If you're not taking a multivitamin, now is the time to start. The Center for Disease Control currently recommends that all women of child-bearing age take a multivitamin with at least 400 micrograms of folic acid to decrease the risk of birth defects that affect a baby's brain and spinal cord. Your doctor may recommend that you take a prescription prenatal vitamin that has a higher level of folic acid.

What to Do When You Can't Conceive

Most couples take the ability to have children for granted. Unless they already know that a defect or injury exists, there's no way for them to know that they will have difficulty conceiving until they try. When they start trying, it can be a shock when conception doesn't occur right away.

The Problem of Infertility

Infertility is usually defined as the inability to conceive or bear a child after a year of unprotected intercourse. It's a common problem, and if you haven't experienced it, you probably know someone who has. Under normal circumstances, there's a 25 percent chance of conception per month for fertile couples having unprotected intercourse.

However, approximately 15 percent of couples will not be able to conceive within a year.

Since the 1990s, the incidence of infertility has been increasing as more couples have postponed childbearing until their mid-forties. As couples age, fertility decreases, mainly due to aging eggs. A female baby is born with roughly 1 to 2 million eggs, many of which are lost through aging and menstrual cycles. The eggs of a woman who attempts to conceive in her forties may not fertilize and divide easily. Older women are also more likely to have conditions that inhibit conception, such as pelvic adhesions or endometriosis (a condition in which the lining of the uterus implants and grows in other places in the pelvis).

Simple Steps You can Take

There are some simple steps you can take to help conception occur. One of the simplest is to chart your menstrual cycles so you can predict when you're going to ovulate. Ovulation usually occurs two weeks before the beginning of your next period. If your cycles are irregular, the timing of ovulation may vary, making conception more difficult. An ovulation predictor kit (available at any pharmacy) could help. Ovulation usually occurs within twenty-four to forty-eight hours after the test shows a positive result. Of course, that's when you would want to have intercourse.

Sometimes having marital relations too frequently can be a problem because it can reduce the sperm count. Around the time of ovulation, it's best to engage in marital intimacy no more than every other day. It's also not a good idea to use artificial lubricants, as they can inhibit sperm activity, and you wouldn't want to jump out of bed or douche immediately afterwards. Despite what some people may tell you, there are no "magic" positions that will ensure conception.

Your husband can help conception occur by avoiding activities that increase his body temperature for extended periods of time, because that can also affect the sperm count. Ask him to postpone that long bicycle trip and spend less time in the Jacuzzi.

Testing and Treatments

If you follow these suggestions and still do not conceive, it may be time to consult a specialist. As a rule, a couple faced with infertility should consult a gynecologist or reproductive endocrinologist after a year of trying to conceive. If one or both of you is older or if you suspect there's a problem, you may want to schedule a visit sooner. Infertility evaluation begins with simple studies and progressively becomes more complex. The majority of the testing is directed toward the wife.

Possible Causes of Infertility

About 20 percent of all married couples seek medical assistance to bear children. About 90 percent of the time the cause of infertility is found. About 35 percent of the time the problem is with the man, and 50 percent of the time it's with the woman. Approximately 5 percent of the time a combination of problems with both partners is the cause. Unfortunately, despite extensive testing, 10 percent of couples tested will not find a reason for their infertility.

In the first step of the evaluation process, your doctor will take a complete medical history and give you a thorough examination. He will look for a history of irregular periods and pelvic infections or surgeries, such as an appendectomy or removal of an ovarian cyst; ask you about your previous methods of conception control and prior pregnancies; and discuss with you at length the intimate details of your marital life, including the timing and frequency of marital intimacy. He'll pay particular attention to your weight, body type, and pelvic region. He'll also ask you questions about your husband's health and arrange for his semen to be analyzed. If it's abnormal, your husband may be referred to a urologist for further evaluation. In all of these things, your doctor is looking for clues to the causes of your infertility.

For a woman, reasons for infertility can include failure to ovulate, hormonal imbalance, and the presence of scar tissue in the fallopian tubes or uterus.

Failure to Ovulate

Your doctor may ask you to keep a Basal Body Temperature chart to find out if and when you're ovulating. You do this by taking your temperature with a regular thermometer first thing in the morning, before you do anything else, including getting out of bed. If you are ovulating, your temperature will be slightly higher in the second half of your cycle. If your cycles are irregular or you're older, your doctor may order blood tests to check for signs of early menopause or thyroid problems.

Hormonal Imbalance

The hormone progesterone, which is high in the second half of your cycle, helps prepare the lining of the uterus to receive a fertilized egg. One week before your period, your doctor may order a blood test to check your hormone level and confirm that ovulation has occurred. Even though your level of progesterone may appear adequate, it may not be sufficient to ensure implantation of a fertilized egg, so a few days before your period your doctor may also ask that an endometrial biopsy be performed to see if the lining of the uterus can sustain implantation.

Tubal or Uterine Scar Tissue

Your doctor may order a hysterosalpingogram, an X-ray evaluation of the uterus and fallopian tubes. Taken after dye is injected through the cervix, this X-ray will reveal any tubal blockage or abnormalities in the uterus. If it doesn't reveal a problem, your doctor may advise you to have a laparoscopy. While you are under general anesthesia, he will make a small incision in your navel and insert a laparoscope, which will allow him to examine your pelvis. About 50 percent of the time, a problem like endometriosis or tubal scarring is found.

Treatment for Infertility

Treatments for infertility are directed at whatever problems are discovered.

Fertility Drugs

If ovulation is not occurring, fertility drugs may be used to induce it. Taking a Clomid (clomiphene citrate) pill for five days each month is the simplest method. Some women receive a daily injection of Pergonal prior to ovulation. The use of both drugs requires careful monitoring. Women need a pelvic examination or ultrasound prior to taking Clomid each month. Pergonal requires even closer monitoring through daily ultrasounds and blood tests. For that reason it is usually only prescribed at infertility centers. If the only problem is with ovulation, 85 percent of the women using these medications will be pregnant within six months. The risks of using them include multiple gestation and ovarian cysts.

Sperm Injection

In the event of a low sperm count, your doctor may inject your husband's sperm directly into your uterus. That requires a visit to his office the day ovulation occurs, which means that ovulation has to be precisely determined through basal body temperature readings, blood or urine tests, or daily pelvic ultrasounds. Your husband will need to collect a semen sample that you can bring with you.[4] The sperm is injected into the uterus by inserting a thin piece of tubing through the cervix. The procedure is simple and involves minimal discomfort.

Surgical Procedures

Further evaluation and treatment becomes much more complex, and your doctor may refer you to an infertility center. If there is tubal blockage from infections or prior tubal ligation, pelvic scarring, or endometriosis, major surgical procedures may be needed. Endometriosis can be treated either surgically with laparoscopy or with gonadotropins-releasing hormone agonists (GnRH agonists) such as Lupron. The pregnancy rate is very low if you have tubal blockage. In this case, you will probably be advised to have In Vitro Fertilization (IVF).

IVF

IVF (In Vitro Fertilization) begins with daily injections of gonadotropins to artificially stimulate the ovaries to produce a greater number of eggs, which are then removed midcycle by either laparoscopy or ultrasound-guided aspiration through the vagina. The eggs are combined with sperm in a laboratory, which means fertilization occurs outside of the body. A few days later, the fertilized eggs are implanted in the uterus or frozen for use in another cycle.

GIFT and ZIFT

Other procedures include Gamete Intrafallopian Transfer (GIFT) and Zygote Intrafallopian Transfer (ZIFT). Like IVF, GIFT involves stimulating the ovaries and removing the eggs by laparoscopy, but instead of fertilizing them in the lab, the eggs and sperm are placed separately in the fallopian tubes, where fertilization occurs naturally. For this to succeed, the fallopian tubes must be normal. GIFT is now performed infrequently because IVF cycles are more precise and the pregnancy rates are higher, but it may be an option for couples who are morally opposed to IVF or other procedures that involve fertilization outside of the body. ZIFT is similar to GIFT, but fertilization occurs in the lab, and the embryo is placed in the fallopian tubes instead of the uterus.

ICSI

Intracytoplasmic Sperm Injection (ICSI) is similar to IVF, but the sperm is injected directly into the ovum under a microscope in the laboratory. Since only one sperm is needed for this procedure, it is usually performed in cases of serious sperm abnormalities.

Counting the Cost

Treatment for infertility can be an emotional and financial strain on couples. The diagnostic procedures and treatments can be very expensive. Costs can run as high as $5,000 to $15,000 for just one month of IVF, and often this is not covered by insurance. You also need to consider the loss of income because of the time you have to take off work for doctor visits and surgical procedures.

The medications used to treat infertility are not only expensive, but can also have unpleasant side effects. Lupron induces a state resembling menopause and may cause hot flashes, vaginal dryness, and thinning of the bones if used for longer than six months. Many of the procedures cause physical discomfort and intrude on the privacy of the couple. Intimacy may become mechanical.

Infertility can sometimes lead to a major life crisis. You may feel very isolated, especially if everyone else you know is having a baby. Everywhere you look—movies, television, magazines, books—you're bombarded with pictures of babies and information about parenting. Family members may inadvertently exert pressure by asking you when you are going to have children, while well-meaning friends often make helpful suggestions like "Relax" or "Go on a vacation." Some even suggest intimate techniques you might try.

If you are pursuing treatment for infertility, try not to have unrealistically high expectations. Although there are many new and sophisticated medical procedures that provide many answers and cures, only about 50 percent of infertile couples seeking help will get pregnant. Conception may occur. But if it doesn't, you will eventually need to come to the point of accepting your infertility.

The inability to have children can be as painful as the loss of a loved one. If you find yourself in that situation, it's very important for you to acknowledge feelings of guilt, anger, and depression as they arise. These problems have deep roots, and you need to understand them so infertility won't control your lives.

While infertility evaluation may bring you the peace of knowing that you did everything humanly possible to have a child, it can also place great strain on the husband-wife relationship. We encourage you not to turn away from each other. Your spouse should be one of your greatest sources of comfort. Remember, too, that the husband and wife relationship is already a complete family unit. Children are welcome additions to the family, but they do not complete it.

Chapter Two

While You're Waiting

So now you're expecting! Congratulations!

Every special event in life deserves thoughtful preparation. While you're waiting for your baby to arrive, you'll need to decide who will be directly involved in your "birth-day" celebration, learn as much as you can about the physical changes going on in both you and your baby, and take some practical steps to get ready for the big day.

Options for Prenatal Care and Delivery

Many factors enter into your choice of a birthing facility and healthcare providers—where you want your baby to be born, your family circumstances and finances (including insurance coverage), and a doctor's knowledge, experience, philosophy, and communication skills. In order to make a wise choice, you should consider all the options that match your preferences and meet your needs.

Birthing Facilities

Other than in the home, policies will vary with regard to medical intervention, length of stay, and choices available. Here are some options to consider.

- *Perinatal unit*: An area designed for high-risk pregnancy, labor, and birth, with advanced medical technology immediately available.

- *LDR*: A single room for labor, delivery, and recovery that provides a homelike environment but still has technology and emergency equipment available. You may be moved to another room for postpartum care.

- *Freestanding birth center*: A building separate from a hospital that may or may not be close to a medical center. The atmosphere is similar to that of an LDR, but minimal technology is available, so you would have to be transferred to a hospital if advanced medical intervention became necessary.

- *Home*: A familiar environment with minimal technology availability. If medical intervention becomes necessary, you would have to be transferred to a hospital.

Health-care Providers

Depending on what kind of insurance you have, you may be able to choose from a range of options.

- *Lay Midwives*: Laypeople, traditionally with no medical training, who have learned how to manage pregnancy, labor, and delivery from others and by experience. They may use herbs and natural remedies as part of their practice, and they might deliver in your home or in a birth center that may or may not have appropriate medical backup available. Lay midwife practice is legal in some states.

• *Certified Nurse-midwives*: Registered nurses with post-graduate training who specialize in prenatal care and deliveries of women with low-risk pregnancies. Like lay midwives, they emphasize natural management and use technology only when necessary. They work closely with medical doctors, including obstetricians, for consultation, co-management, and referral. Options for the place of delivery include high- and low-risk labor and delivery units in the hospital with an obstetrician available; in-hospital or freestanding birth centers; or in your home.

• *General/Family Practitioners*: Medical doctors (MDs) with broad training in many fields of medicine, including obstetrics. Their experience in managing pregnancy, labor, and delivery will vary according to their individual training, and they might use an obstetrician as a consultant. They deliver babies in low-risk labor and delivery units in hospitals, in freestanding and hospital birth centers, or in homes.

• *Obstetricians*: MDs who have completed a four-year post-graduate residency in obstetrics and gynecology and are experienced in managing high- and low-risk pregnancies, labor, and deliveries. Their philosophies of care vary, as do the places where they deliver babies. Traditionally, most have preferred high- and low-risk labor and delivery units in hospitals.

• *Perinatologists*: MDs who have completed a residency in obstetrics and gynecology and have an additional two to three years of training in high-risk obstetrics. Specializing in high-risk pregnancies, they follow their patients throughout their pregnancies and act as consultants to other doctors. Since they emphasize medical intervention for problem pregnancies, they deliver babies in labor and delivery units in hospitals.[5]

In addition to a primary health-care provider, you'll need to choose a labor support-person, or "coach." This person helps set the tone for your emotional response to childbirth, so it's very important to select someone who is sensitive—someone who knows when to speak a kind word and when to remain silent, when to touch you and when to respect your way of dealing with pain. A good coach will recognize that for a woman in labor, time stands still.

What's Going On?

Even before you were aware that you were pregnant, many changes were taking place in your body—and there will be lots more in the months ahead! The more you know about what's going on in your body, the better prepared you'll be to cope with these changes as they come.

First Trimester

Imagine all the changes that take place in you and your baby during the first fourteen weeks of pregnancy! By the fourth week, all the basic structures of your baby's major organs are forming. By the twenty-fifth day, his heart is beating, and by the eighth week his brain and spinal cord have formed. During weeks nine through twelve, he nearly doubles in size, and at around twelve weeks, his internal sex organs are identifiable. At the end of the first trimester, his arms, hands, fingers, feet, and toes are forming. He is approximately three inches in length and weighs one ounce.

During this first trimester, your body goes through dramatic changes as well. By the twelfth week, the placenta is producing the hormones needed to maintain your pregnancy. Because each woman and each pregnancy is unique, some women may experience many of the following symptoms early in pregnancy, while others may experience very few.

- increased fatigue
- breast changes—fullness, tenderness, darkening of the areolae, and tingling sensations
- nausea, with or without vomiting
- frequent urination
- indigestion or heartburn
- constipation
- food cravings and dislikes
- bloating
- mood swings and irritability

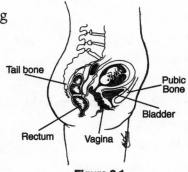

Figure 2.1

Second Trimester

As you move into the second trimester (fourteen to twenty-six weeks), hair begins to grow on your baby's scalp. His finger and toenail beds are forming, as are his eyebrows and eyelashes. He can suck his thumb and swallow. If the baby is a girl, by the sixteenth week her ovaries are formed and each ovary contains eggs. A cheesy substance (*vernix caseosa*) covers the baby's body, protecting his sensitive skin from drying out in the amniotic environment. You will feel your baby move, stretch, and kick during this trimester. By weeks twenty-six to twenty-eight, the baby measures thirteen to fifteen inches and may weigh as much as two-and-a-half pounds.

The good news for most women is that nausea and vomiting, frequent urination, and tenderness of the breasts decrease or disappear during the second trimester. The bad news is that many of the other first-trimester pregnancy symptoms may continue. In addition, these symptoms may appear:

- bloating, heartburn, and indigestion
- increase in appetite
- enlargement of the breasts
- varicose veins in the legs
- hemorrhoids
- noticeable veins in the breasts
- occasional mild headaches
- nasal stuffiness
- heaviness in the lower abdomen
- lower backaches
- leg cramps
- itchy skin, especially on the abdomen

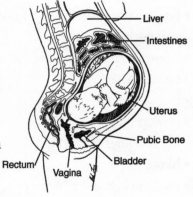

Figure 2.3

Third Trimester

Weeks twenty-seven to forty put the finishing touches on the Creator's masterpiece. Your baby's eyes open, close, and blink, and he can sense a difference between light and dark. His ears can respond to sound, and his taste buds can distinguish between sweet and sour. Rapid brain growth is occurring, and at the end of the seventh month, it controls rhythmic breathing and body temperature. Fat cells form under your baby's skin and help smooth out his wrinkles. He grimaces, curls up, yawns, and stretches. By weeks thirty-eight to forty, the average baby is twenty inches long and weighs seven to eight pounds.

As the third trimester progresses, the increasing weight of the baby may cause you lower back, lower abdominal, and pelvic discomfort. Other symptoms of the third trimester may include:

- Braxton-Hicks contractions (intermittent contractions of the uterus)
- mild swelling (edema) in the hands, ankles, and feet
- increased fatigue
- increased indigestion and heartburn
- constipation and hemorrhoids
- leg cramps and varicose veins
- difficulty sleeping and resting
- increasing frequency of urination
- shortness of breath
- colostrum leaking from breasts
- itchy skin, especially on the abdomen
- stretch marks
- increase in vaginal discharge

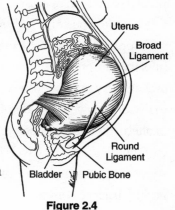

Figure 2.4

By this time you'll probably be getting impatient. You'll want the waiting to end and the parenting to begin! But there are still some things to do while you're waiting.

Have You Thought About?

You're pregnant. You have a due date. What now? There is some planning to be done and decisions to be made before your baby arrives. Here are some things to consider.

Devise a Birth Plan

Although the vast majority of pregnancies result in normal, healthy children, a small percentage have unexpected outcomes. So even as you anticipate a normal process of pregnancy, delivery, and recovery, it's wise to be aware of the variations in labor and the options available to you.

Between 8 and 20 percent of low-risk pregnancies require some form of medical intervention. That means you should prepare yourself for both the best and worst scenarios and be willing to adjust your plans if some kind of medical intervention becomes necessary to provide a healthy outcome for you and your baby.

Appendix C, "Labor Variations and Options," provides detailed information on variations in labor and delivery and the options available to you. Once you familiarize yourself with it, you'll be ready to decide how you would feel most comfortable and which medical or alternative interventions you want, if any. Discuss your plans with everyone who will be actively involved so they will know how to help support you in labor and birth. As you plan, seek to maintain a healthy balance between respect for birth as a natural physiological process and the need for appropriate medical intervention.

Select a Pediatrician

You should choose a pediatrician by the eighth month of your pregnancy. If the baby is born before you have made a decision, your obstetrician will refer you to one for the baby's initial evaluation in the hospital. Here are some action steps you can take to help you make your choice:

• Evaluate your insurance coverage to determine which doctor you can select.

- Get recommendations from other mothers.
- Get a referral list from your obstetrician.
- Get a list of pediatricians who have admitting privileges at the hospital.
- Consider the location of the pediatrician's office.
- If possible, interview several pediatricians before making a decision.

Here are some questions to ask during an interview:
- What are your office hours?
- Are evening or weekend appointments available?
- What are your billing arrangements?
- How often are well-baby checkups?
- How soon will you see a sick child?
- Will you see a sick child outside of your normal business hours?
- Will you see more than one sick child in the family at the same time?
- Will you prescribe medication over the telephone?
- When you aren't on call, who takes over for you?
- Can we contact you if we have questions about a treatment proposed by the secondary pediatrician?

Remember: A good pediatrician takes time to teach parents about their children's health and is open to questions, not intimidated by them. There should be mutual trust and respect between you and your baby's doctor.

Stock Up

Start stocking up on items you will need prior to the baby's arrival early, before it becomes a difficult chore, and try to have it done by the eighth month. Take advantage of sales, and have enough on hand to last for six to eight weeks after the baby arrives. Starting around the seventh month, make double portions when you prepare meals and freeze the extra in disposable containers. Purchase your postpartum supplies early. Most dads feel uncomfortable buying them. If you're going to use using disposable diapers, have plenty on hand. New babies go through them very quickly—forty-eight to ninety-six diapers a week! Complete the baby's basic layette by the eighth month, and have all linens and clothing washed before his due date.

Pack Your Suitcases

You never know when your baby is going to be born. He may arrive four weeks early or two weeks late. Therefore, we suggest that you pack your suitcases three to four weeks before the baby's due date. You should pack three of them: a labor bag to take with you to the hospital at the onset of labor, a mother's bag for someone to bring to the hospital after the baby arrives, and a baby's bag for the trip home. If you're a first-time mom, you might need to know what to pack. Here are some suggestions:

Labor Bag
- video and camera equipment (extra film, tapes, batteries)
- special pillow, if needed
- battery-powered tape recorder and tapes to record your baby's first sounds
- money for phone calls or a cell phone
- list of business and home phone numbers
- hand mirror
- lightweight robe, slippers, socks
- lip balm, lotion, sour lollipops

- snacks for your labor coach
- time passers: books, magazines, playing cards
- rolling pin, tennis balls in a sock for relieving back pain
- labor flowchart

Mother's Bag

- two nightgowns (nursing type if breast-feeding)
- robe, slippers, socks
- three to five pairs of maternity underwear
- one or two nursing bras with nursing pads
- toothbrush and toothpaste, deodorant, soap, makeup, perfume, shampoo, and hair supplies
- announcements, stationery, stamps, thank-you notes, and baby book
- address book with phone numbers
- leisure reading, magazines, hobby supplies
- outfit for going home (maternity clothes are most comfortable)

Baby's Bag

- outfit for going home (bring two in case one is soiled)
- socks and undershirt
- receiving blanket
- spit-up rag and diapers
- sweater and hat, depending on the weather

Note: You must have an adequate car seat available for the baby's trip home. A soft, cushioned head support is also a good idea.

Finalize Your Birth Plan

Tour the hospital maternity ward by the eighth month of your pregnancy, and complete the admission papers for the hospital two to three weeks before your due date. Review your birth plan and discuss it with each of your doctors early in the eighth month. Be realistic and flexible. Review the hospital's policies regarding the options available for labor, delivery, and recovery, and discuss any concerns and questions you have about circumcision with both your doctor and pediatrician.

Arrange for Help

You'll need help for at least the first few days at home after the baby arrives. It may be the new father, relatives, a neighbor, or experienced hired help. Think about the basic chores that will need to be done, and list the ones others can do (for example, basic housework, vacuuming, cooking, laundry). Discuss how to get help, how long it will need to be available, and then make arrangements for it.

Think Ahead

Complete a "to call" list. Include both business and home numbers. Anticipate special occasions, such as your mother's birthday, that will occur from one month before, to two months after the baby's due date. Shop ahead for gifts, cards, and wrapping paper. Schedule all your major cleaning projects so they'll be done when your baby arrives, and work at completing them slowly so you don't feel rushed toward the end of your pregnancy.

Personalize the Birth Experience

If you would like a visual record of the labor or birth, find out if the hospital allows it, and then put someone who is not actively participating in the delivery in charge of recording it. If you want special music, make sure a tape or CD player with working batteries is available. Consider creating or perpetuating special family traditions, such as taking pictures or sharing a meal together after the baby is born.

Watch for Warning Signs

The following symptoms may indicate potential problems or complications.

- dizziness or fainting spells
- persistent nausea and vomiting
- severe or persistent headache or other pain
- blurred vision or other visual disturbances
- swelling of the face or eyes
- pronounced swelling of the hands or feet
- sudden weight gain
- loss of fluid from the vagina
- bleeding from the vagina
- vaginal discharge that is irritating
- sore or blister in vaginal area
- painful, reddened, swollen, hot area in the calf or area behind the knee
- fever
- burning or pain upon urinating
- significant decrease in amount of urination
- more than four to five contractions per hour before the thirty-sixth week
- major decrease in the movement of the baby

If you experience any of these symptoms, don't wait for the problem to disappear or get worse. Contact your doctor without delay!

Chapter Three

Prenatal Testing

*T*aking tests. There will be plenty of them when you're pregnant. You will be less anxious about the tests that may come your way when you know what they are for and why they are done. In this chapter we describe some of the tests your doctor may advise you to have before the birth of your baby. Although testing can provide you with lots of information, sometimes too much information can cause stress, especially when it isn't conclusive. Some of these tests also have risks associated with them. To keep from becoming anxious, try to learn everything you can about them so that you can weigh their risks and benefits and make a wise decision about which are right for you.

Cystic Fibrosis Carrier Testing

Cystic Fibrosis is a genetic disease in which thick secretions are produced in the lungs and digestive system, leading to chronic lung infections, digestive difficulties, and Diabetes. The average life span of people with Cystic Fibrosis is into the mid-thirties. Both parents have to be carriers of the disease for a child to be born with it. You can be a carrier even if you have no symptoms and no one in your family has it.

Carrier testing has recently become available, and it is now recommended that pregnant women or couples planning to have children be tested. Knowing that your child has or could have Cystic Fibrosis enables you to treat him before problems begin to occur. It's a simple blood test, with no risks involved.

Ultrasound

In this procedure, sound-waves are bounced off the internal structures of both you and your baby and translated into an image on a TV-like screen attached to a computer. They reveal the size, position, and condition of the baby and the placenta, the amount of amniotic fluid present, and the number of babies in your uterus.

If you have a transabdominal ultrasound, you'll lie on your back, and your doctor will apply a gel-type lotion or mineral oil to your abdomen and then rub a transducer across it. You may be instructed to arrive for testing with a full bladder so your uterus will be more visible. Early in your pregnancy, you may have a vaginal ultrasound. In that case, a small transducer will be introduced vaginally, and the ultrasound image will be viewed just as it is in a transabdominal ultrasound.

A detailed high-resolution ultrasound includes 3-D imaging and evaluation of the blood flow to your uterus and in your baby. This type of ultrasound, usually performed by a perinatologist, is rare in low-risk pregnancies, although it will often be done before an amniocentesis (see below) if there is a family history of birth defects, or if a routine ultrasound has revealed an abnormality.

Although there are no documented risks associated with the use of ultrasound in pregnancy, it's still a medical procedure, and it isn't a good idea to have one just so you can "get a look" at your baby.

Triple Screen

This blood test, performed sixteen to eighteen weeks into your pregnancy, assesses your levels of the pregnancy hormone Human Chorionic Gonadotropin (HCG); Estriol, a type of estrogen; and Alpha Fetoprotein (AFP), a protein excreted by the developing baby into the amniotic fluid, a small amount of which leaks into your bloodstream. These levels are compared to the risk for your age to predict your chance of having a baby with Down Syndrome or another chromosomal problem. A triple screen can detect as much as 60 percent of Down Syndrome. High levels may indicate Spina Bifida (a defect in the Spinal Column) or anencephaly (the absence of part or all of the brain).

There are several other conditions that can cause the AFP to be abnormal, such as kidney problems and protrusion of the umbilical cord into the abdomen. If the level is abnormal, your doctor will recommend further testing, including a detailed high-resolution ultrasound by a perinatologist and possibly an amniocentesis.

Amniocentesis

The amniotic fluid contains fetal cells that can be examined for chromosomal abnormalities in the baby, elevated AFP levels, and the L/S (lecithin and sphingomyelin) ratio, which reveals the maturity of the baby's lungs. There are two types of amniocentesis: a genetic amnio, which takes place between the sixteenth and eighteenth week of pregnancy, and a maturity amnio, which is performed late in the third trimester to determine if the baby's lungs are mature.

During this procedure, you lie on your back with your head slightly elevated while your abdomen is cleansed and covered with sterile drapes. The baby and the placenta are located by ultrasound, a small amount of local anesthetic is injected into the skin of your abdomen, and a long, hollow needle is inserted. Ultrasound guides the needle to prevent injury to you or your baby, and a small amount of amniotic fluid is removed for testing. Results are received two weeks after a genetic amnio or from four to twenty-four hours after a maturity amnio. Risks for a genetic amnio include miscarriage, injury to the baby, and injury to the placenta. Maturity amnios can injure the placenta and cause premature labor. The chance of losing your baby due to an amniocentesis is a little less than one in two-hundred.

Chorionic Villi Sampling (CVS)

Chorionic villi are fingerlike projections in the tissue surrounding the baby that contain his genetic makeup. Between the tenth and twelfth weeks of pregnancy, using ultrasound as a guide, the doctor inserts a small catheter through the vagina into the uterus and removes a small amount of tissue, which is then evaluated for chromosomal irregularities. It can also be performed abdominally like an amniocentesis. You'll receive the final results of the test in one to three weeks, though a preliminary result may be available within a few days. Risks associated with this procedure include infection, damage to the developing baby, and miscarriage. Pregnancy loss rates are generally just slightly greater than for amniocentesis.

Diabetic Screening

This is a blood test done between the twenty-sixth and twenty-eighth weeks of your pregnancy to determine if you have developed gestational Diabetes. You will be instructed to drink a pre-measured amount of a highly concentrated sugar solution (glucola), and an hour later a blood sample will be drawn to measure blood glucose levels. If the levels are elevated, your doctor may perform a full glucose tolerance test. There are no risks associated with this procedure.

Fetal Movement Counting

Studies have indicated a possible correlation between a decrease in movement of the baby and fetal distress. The purpose of this test, which can be performed after the twenty-eighth week of pregnancy, is to count the movements of the baby within a specific amount of time.

Fetal movement counting involves no risk. In fact, it's a good idea for all pregnant women to do this routinely. Approximately three times a week, after a meal lie down on your left side, and count the number of times your baby moves in a two-hour period. Generally, ten kicks are considered normal. You don't need to worry if your baby is kicking fewer times than that, because he could be sleeping. Nevertheless, it's a good idea to let your doctor know. He might want to do additional testing. If you don't feel any movement within a period of twenty-four hours, tell your doctor right away.

Beta Strep Culture

In the early 1970s, the bacteria group beta streptococcus (GBS) was identified as the number one cause of life-threatening infections in newborn babies. These bacteria are found in the vagina and/or lower intestine of between 15 to 20 percent of all healthy women. Women who test positive for GBS are said to be "colonized." GBS usually causes infant illness within the first seven days of life, but infections can occur at up to three months of age.

Most often, GBS colonizes the baby during labor either by traveling upward from the mother's vagina into the uterus, or by infecting the baby as he passes through the birth canal. Illness occurs when the bacteria enters the baby's bloodstream. This can then lead to shock, pneumonia, and meningitis (an infection of the baby's spinal fluid and brain tissue). All of these conditions are life-threatening.

Since a GBS infection can be prevented with early detection, many doctors routinely screen for it by doing cultures on the mother in the third trimester of pregnancy. These cultures can be taken from the vagina, rectum, cervix, or urine. If they know that you are colonized, they will give you antibiotics during labor as a preventive measure.

The culture involves no risk to you or your baby, and it helps to know if you are colonized. If you've had previous rapid labors, you'll need to get to the hospital early in labor to allow time for the administration of antibiotics.

Fetal Fibronectin

During an exam near the end of pregnancy, a swab is taken from the vaginal secretions behind the cervix to test for fibronectin, a protein found in the vaginal secretions of a woman near term. This test is useful for someone at risk of delivering prematurely because it can help predict preterm labor. It is most helpful when the results are negative; that is, when they indicate that delivery is not likely to occur within two weeks. Positive results are not as accurate, although they can signal the need for continued monitoring for preterm labor.

Nonstress Testing

This is a simple, non-invasive test done anytime in the third trimester to evaluate the well-being of the baby in cases where there is poor fetal movement, signs of difficulty with the mother, the baby is overdue, or the mother is over thirty-five or has medical problems such as Diabetes or Hypertension.

An external fetal monitor will be applied to your abdomen to record your baby's heart rate, and you will be instructed to record his movements. When he moves, his heart rate should accelerate. He is considered reactive if there are two movements within twenty minutes. If he is not reactive (a baby can be non-reactive because he's sleeping or has a low blood-sugar level), or his heart rate decreases, your doctor may follow up with further testing. There is no known risk.

Biophysical Profile

This profile consists of five evaluations of your baby's well-being in the uterus. The first component is the nonstress test discussed above. The next three are assessments of fetal breathing movements, motion, and tone, all of which are evaluated through ultrasound. Positive responses for these three components include thirty-second episodes of breathing movements in a thirty-minute period, three fetal movements in a thirty-minute period, and the baby's return to a flexed position after a period of movement. In the fifth measurement, ultrasound is used to determine if the amount of amniotic fluid is adequate.

Each component is given a total score of two points. Eight to ten points indicate normal to good. Four to seven points indicate borderline, and the test may be repeated the following day. Zero to three points indicate that the doctor may have to consider delivering the baby immediately. There are no known risks.

Contraction Stress Test, or Oxytocin Challenge Test (OCT)

This test, given just prior to delivery or if you are overdue, is used to assess your baby's ability to respond to the strenuous demands of labor. An external fetal monitor and an external uterine monitor are attached to you to monitor uterine contractions, which are elicited either by stimulating your nipples or by an intravenous infusion of oxytocin (Pitocin). The baby's responses to the contractions are monitored.

If the placenta is covering the cervix, this test could induce preterm labor or cause vaginal bleeding. Occasionally, the Pitocin infusion can cause stress and result in a false reading.

Mastering the technical aspects of prenatal testing can be challenging, but the more you know about them, the better prepared you'll be to evaluate your doctor's recommendations and decide which tests are right and necessary for you and your baby. Some decisions will most likely be easy; others may be very difficult. In either case, be sure you have all the facts. Knowing that you have made an informed decision will help relieve your anxiety.

Chapter Four

The Importance of Self-Care

Taking care of yourself during pregnancy is so essential that we're devoting an entire chapter to it. Why is self-care so important? Because your baby is *completely* dependent upon you for all his needs. While good prenatal care is a must, ultimately *you* are responsible for providing the best environment possible for your developing baby. Eating right, managing your weight, exercising regularly, and taking steps to relieve the common discomforts of pregnancy are all parts of good self-care.

Eating Right

What you eat is directly related to your baby's growth. That's why it's important to eat a balanced diet. Specifically, every day you should eat three to four servings (or 60 grams) of protein, five to nine servings of a variety of fruits and vegetables, six to eight servings of breads and grains (be sure to eat ones that are high in fiber—they help prevent constipation), and four to six servings of milk products. This sounds like a lot, but it really isn't when you remember that a serving is usually only four ounces, or half a cup.

The total calcium requirement during pregnancy is 1200 to 1500 milligrams a day. If you find you aren't eating enough dairy products, you may want to take a calcium supplement. Your doctor can recommend one for you. In general, you shouldn't take more than 500 milligrams at one time.

If you have a problem eating enough protein, here are some ways to increase your intake:

- Add cheese to sandwiches, casseroles, snacks, and eggs (cottage cheese is also an excellent source of protein, although it isn't as high in calcium as milk or yogurt).
- Add sunflower seeds or other nuts to sandwich spreads and egg or chicken salad.
- Keep trail mix on hand for snacking (use low-fat granola and nuts).
- Add nonfat dry milk to casseroles, hamburgers, and meatloaf, and combine it with fresh fruit, ice, and yogurt to make shakes (you could also add protein powder).

It's hard to overstate the importance of drinking lots of water. You need to drink six to eight glasses a day. That can seem like a lot, but if you make it a habit, you'll soon see that it actually makes you feel better. It helps your body keep up with the increase in blood volume during pregnancy and can also help prevent bladder infections and relieve muscle cramping and headaches.

Coffee intake, on the other hand, should be limited. There is some evidence that drinking it early in pregnancy may increase the chance of miscarriage. (Caffeine is present in many over-the-counter products, so be sure to check the labels.) Don't drink alcohol at all. No level of intake is considered safe during pregnancy.

You should not eat raw or undercooked eggs, meat, or fish. That means no dinners out at your favorite sushi bar unless they use cooked seafood. Recently the FDA has warned pregnant women to avoid eating fish high in mercury. These are primarily large ocean fish such as shark, swordfish, king mackerel, tuna, and tilefish. Shellfish, smaller ocean fish, or farm-raised fish such as salmon are safe to eat.

Also avoid soft cheeses, as they may contain the bacteria Listeria, which can lead to miscarriage. Most of the problem has been with soft cheeses from Mexico, but it is best to avoid all soft cheeses, including feta, Brie, Camembert, blue cheese, and cheese made with unpasteurized milk.

If you didn't begin taking prenatal vitamins before you became pregnant, start now and take them throughout your pregnancy and for as long as you nurse. This will provide the folic acid you need, as well as the supplemental iron needed to increase the volume of blood in both you and your baby. Keep in mind that a vitamin supplement is just that—a supplement. Taking one cannot take the place of eating a balanced diet.

Just as you shouldn't take any medications (including over-the-counter ones) without your doctor's approval, you shouldn't take additional vitamins without discussing it with him, as high doses of certain vitamins (Vitamin A, for instance) are linked to birth defects and can have other toxic effects on a developing baby. You should also avoid the use of all herbal products during pregnancy.

Managing Your Weight

Weight gain during pregnancy can be a source of concern for some women. Average weight gain during pregnancy is between twenty-four and twenty-eight pounds, distributed as follows:

Baby	7.5 pounds
Placenta	1.0 pounds
Amniotic fluid	2.0 pounds
Uterus (weight increase)	2.5 pounds
Breast tissue	3.0 pounds
Blood volume	4.0 pounds
Maternal stores	4.0–8.0 pounds

The average woman gains about ten pounds in the first half of pregnancy and approximately one pound a week in the second half.

Too little weight gain can increase the risk of intrauterine growth retardation of the fetus, while too much weight gain can increase the risk of Diabetes and Hypertension. Gaining too much weight can also increase the baby's weight and lead to a more difficult delivery and the possible need for a Cesarean Section. If you were overweight before you became pregnant, you may need to gain only fifteen to twenty-five pounds. If you were underweight, you may need to gain thirty to forty. Be sure to ask your doctor what he thinks is an appropriate weight gain for you.

As the old saying goes, you are "eating for two"—but that doesn't necessarily mean in amount. You need only three hundred calories more than what you would normally eat each day to maintain your weight goals. That isn't really a lot. There may be certain times during your pregnancy when your appetite increases and you gain more weight than expected. Often this signals a growth spurt in the baby. Other times, especially late in pregnancy, you may find that your appetite is much less. Often women don't gain much weight in the last month. If your weight gain has been good up to that point and you're eating smaller amounts of good foods, this is usually not a cause for concern. Your baby is still growing.

You may find that you gain too much weight even without eating excessively. Part of this may be due to fluid retention, and part may be due to decreased physical activity, especially if you have been put on bed-rest. This can be discouraging, but whatever you do—don't diet! If you are watching what you eat and exercising as you are able to, you're doing what's best for your baby.

Exercising Regularly

Exercising during pregnancy has many benefits. It helps prepare your body for both ongoing bodily changes and the labor process, which will place special demands on it; it has been shown to shorten labor and decrease the risk of fetal distress in labor; it can help you control your weight and decrease your chance of developing Diabetes; and it can help alleviate some of the discomforts of pregnancy and give you an emotional boost.

With all that said, pregnancy is not the time to *begin* a regimen of strenuous exercise. If you haven't been exercising regularly, the best thing to do is to start walking. You might want to begin by taking a twenty-minute walk daily, and then increase to thirty minutes. Swimming is also an excellent exercise during pregnancy.

If you exercised regularly before you became pregnant, you can probably continue, but with modifications. The ligaments around joints loosen during pregnancy, so you need to do stretching exercises carefully. You also need to take care to avoid injury. Avoid high-risk activities like downhill skiing, ice hockey, and horse-back riding.

Here are some prenatal exercises you can safely do, as well as an explanation of how to do them and the benefits they provide. Check with your doctor before you begin doing any kind of exercise. At the beginning of each exercise session, take the time to do some gentle stretching. Avoid exercising lying flat on your back for an extended period, as this can make you dizzy when you sit up.

Kegel Exercise

• Strengthens your perineal/pelvic floor muscles.

• The Kegel exercise can be illustrated in the following manner: During urination, stop the flow of urine, and then relax, allowing the flow to continue. The muscles you used to stop the flow are the pelvic floor muscles. Tighten these muscles for ten seconds, and then relax. Do these exercises in sets of ten to fifteen, completing five to ten sets every day.

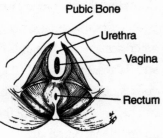

**Figure 4.1
Pelvic Floor Muscles**

Shoulder Rotation

• Relieves upper backache.

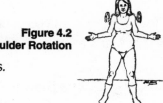

**Figure 4.2
Shoulder Rotation**

• Shrug shoulders in circular motions.

Leg Bend

• Relieves round ligament pain (round ligaments support the uterus in the pelvis).

• When you're experiencing sharp abdominal pain on one side, lift and bend the leg on that side and hold for a count of ten. You can also do this lying down or by using a chair or step to support your bent leg.

**Figure 4.3
Leg Bend**

Pelvic Rock

• Relieves lower back pain.

**Figure 4.4a
Pelvic Rock**

**Figure 4.4b
Variation of
Pelvic Rock**

• Get down on all fours and gently rotate your hips toward your back, and then release. Be careful not to arch your back. Or, lying on your back with your knees bent, press your lower back onto the floor by tucking in your buttocks. Relax and repeat. This variation is not encouraged after the twentieth week because it may cause depression of the large veins that return the blood to the heart and decrease blood flow to the uterus.

Side Tilt

Figure 4.5
Side Tilt

• Relieves rib cage pressure.

• You can do this exercise in a sitting or standing position. Lift your arm on the side that has the pressure in the rib cage, and then bend it over your head and stretch sideways.

Figure 4.6
Calf Stretch

Calf Stretch

• Relieves lower leg cramps.

• Extend your arms forward and lean on a wall. Extend one leg behind you, hold your heel down on the floor, and lean into the wall.

Ankle Rotation

• Increases circulation to your feet and decreases swelling in your feet and ankles.

• Extend your leg forward and move your foot in curricular motions by rotating it at the ankle.

Figure 4.7
Ankle Rotation

Squatting

• Relieves back and leg aches.

• Squat down with your knees wide apart and lean forward.

Figure 4.8
Squatting

Tailor Press

- Relaxes your inner thigh and pelvic muscles.

- Sit on the floor with your knees spread and the bottoms of your feet touching. Press your knees to the floor for a count of ten, and then relax.

Figure 4.9
Tailor Press

Leg Stretch

- Relieves leg cramps and strengthens back muscles

- Sit with your back straight, your legs extended straight out, and your hands on your thighs. As you slowly lean forward, slide your hands along your legs toward your feet, and hold for a count of ten. Return to starting position.

Figure 4.10
Leg Stretch

Relieving Common Discomforts of Pregnancy

Certain symptoms are considered common in pregnancy. Not all women experience all of them, but most women experience at least some. While not life-threatening, they can cause you discomfort and affect your emotional outlook. Here are some simple things you can do at home to relieve them.

Fatigue

- Adjust your daily schedule to allow for needed rest. Take short naps when possible.
- Eat properly.
- Exercise regularly.

Headache

- Get adequate rest and sleep, eat frequent nutritious meals, and drink plenty of fluids.
- Eliminate or decrease exposure to possible causes of headaches— bright or fluorescent lights, cigarette smoke, loud music or noise, and caffeinated beverages.
- Apply a cool washcloth to the back of your neck and your forehead.
- Massage your neck and shoulder muscles.
- Take a brisk walk, open the windows, and get fresh air if possible.

Backache

- Exercise daily.
- Use good posture, avoid lifting heavy objects, and lift using your legs (bend your knees, not your back).
- Avoid standing for long periods of time. Wear low-heeled shoes with good support.
- Do prenatal exercises frequently. The pelvic tilt works well to relieve back discomfort.
- Use a special maternity support (available at maternity stores) to help take some of the pressure off your back.

Morning Sickness

Morning sickness is a basic condition of pregnancy and common among more than half of all pregnant women. It derives its title from the single fact that the feeling of nausea usually occurs in the morning. Call your health care provider if morning sickness does not improve after sixteen weeks and make sure that you do not become dehydrated from the experience. Call your doctor if vomiting results in weight loss greater than two pounds, or you are vomiting blood or material that looks like coffee grounds. Here are some other helpful suggestions to reduce the discomfort level of morning sickness.

• Change your positions slowly; avoid sudden movements.
• Increase the amount of protein in your diet.
• Avoid greasy, fatty foods.
• Eat several small meals throughout the day; avoid large, heavy meals.
• Drink liquids between meals, not during meals.
• Exercise daily and get fresh air if possible.
• Avoid offensive odors (smelling a fresh lemon often helps mask odors).
• Drink ginger tea or ginger ale, or eat candied ginger (don't take ginger capsules, though).
• Keep crackers by your bed, and eat several about ten minutes before you get out of bed in the morning.

Heartburn and Indigestion
• Eat several small meals each day; avoid spicy and greasy foods.
• Drink plenty of fluids.
• Do not eat or drink within two hours of bedtime.

- Sleep with your head elevated.
- Use correct posture, especially when sitting.
- Ask your doctor about taking antacids.

Constipation

- Eat a well-balanced diet, rich in protein and high-fiber foods. Eat fresh vegetables and fruits. Prunes, prune juice, and bran cereals are very helpful.
- Eat frequent, small meals.
- Avoid straining during bowel movements. Elevate your feet on a stool or box to reduce straining.
- Drink plenty of fluids daily.
- Exercise daily.
- Use stool softeners (available at any drugstore), but avoid taking laxatives unless your doctor says it's okay.

Being good to yourself while you are pregnant means that you are also being good to your baby. Eating right, exercising as appropriate, managing your weight, and handling discomfort as it arises can keep you upbeat and in the best possible physical condition. When at last it's time to deliver your baby, both you and baby will be ready, for in taking care of yourself, you will have also taken care of him.

Chapter Five

It's Time!

None of us knows when the exact time that labor will commence, and when it does, we can not predict what it will be like or what the outcome will be. In situations like this, our natural tendency is to be fearful. That's why it is essential that you understand what is going on during labor. Such knowledge is comforting. The more you understand and anticipate the less you are faced with surprises. Knowing what to expect better prepares you for the rigors of labor and delivery. Knowledge is your road map to the final destination.

Signs of the Onset of Labor

As we have each been uniquely created, so each pregnancy and birth is different. Not all women will experience all of these signs of the onset of labor, but again it is helpful to know what kinds of things to expect.

Lightening

An interesting term, "lightening" refers to when the baby drops as his head descends into the pelvis. When it occurs, you may find it easier to breathe and perhaps get some relief from heartburn, but you may also feel more pressure on your rectum and bladder, which may mean more frequent trips to the bathroom. Lightening may occur two to four weeks before delivery with a first-time mom, but for those who have previously given birth, it may not occur until labor has begun.

Increase in Vaginal Secretions

You may notice that normal vaginal secretions have increased. They should not have a foul odor.

Loss of the Mucous Plug, or "Bloody Show"

Before labor begins, there may be an increased mucous vaginal discharge mixed with a slight amount of blood from broken capillaries in the dilating cervix. It can be so slight that you may not even notice it.

Spontaneous Rupture of the Bag of Water

This is one of those things that women worry about the most, because they're afraid that it might happen at the grocery store or some other inconvenient place. Most of the time, though, women are well into the active phase of labor before they experience this gush of fluid from ruptured membranes. If you aren't already at the hospital when this happens, pay attention to the color and odor of the fluid and promptly contact your doctor for instructions. Don't take a tub bath or place anything in your vagina. If you aren't sure if your bag is leaking, lie down for twenty to thirty minutes with your knees up. If you notice a trickle of fluid when you get up, contact your doctor.

Spurt of Energy

As tempting as it is to try to get "one more thing" done, save your energy and use this time to rest. You'll need this extra energy to prepare you for and sustain you through labor and delivery.

Increased Frequency of Braxton-Hicks Contractions

These are those intermittent uterine contractions you may have been feeling for several months now. Though they probably haven't caused you much discomfort to this point, they may become more painful now that you're nearing the end of your pregnancy. Now is a good time to learn how to time contractions so you'll know if you're really in labor. Begin to focus on the frequency, duration, and intensity of the contractions, and ask yourself three questions:

- *How far apart are they?* Measure them from the beginning of one contraction to the beginning of the next.

- *How long do they last?* Measure from the beginning of the contraction to the end of the same contraction.

- *How intense are they?* The abdomen will feel firmer to the touch during a contraction as intensity increases. Are they mild, moderate, or strong?

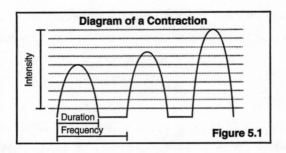

Figure 5.1

Signs That Labor is Premature (before week thirty-six)

The only way you can know for certain that labor—the dilation and effacement of the cervix—has begun prematurely is to have a vaginal exam. Notify your doctor immediately if you experience any of the following symptoms before the thirty-sixth week of your pregnancy:

- menstrual-like cramping, perhaps accompanied by diarrhea or nausea
- a feeling of pressure or aching in the pelvic area, groin, or upper thighs
- dull lower-back pain that is different from the normal back discomfort of pregnancy
- increase in vaginal discharge, especially if it is watery or blood-tinged

Signs That it's False Labor

Unfortunately, there are times when it may be difficult to distinguish true from false labor. If in doubt, call your doctor. Here's a chart that can help you know what to look for.

True vs. False Labor

Indicator	True Labor	False Labor

Contractions
  Intensity
  Duration
  Frequency
  Location
	Increasing
	Increasing
	Increasing
	Usually felt first in lower back and the abdomen
		Unchanged
		Unchanged
		Irregular
		Often felt only in the top of the uterus

Change in activity	Either does not change contractions, or causes an increase in intensity, frequency, and duration	May cause contractions to cease or decrease in intensity, frequency, and duration
Change in cervix	Effacement and dilation are occurring	No cervical changes caused by contractions themselves
Bloody show	May be present	Is not present

Long before your baby is due, ask your doctor when you should go to the hospital or birth center. As a rule, you should go:

- if the membranes have ruptured
- if you aren't feeling the baby move
- if there is vaginal bleeding as in a menstrual period
- if contractions are present before the thirty-sixth week of pregnancy
- if contractions are three to five minutes apart and you're a first-time mom at term
- if you've been down this road before and contractions are five to ten minutes apart at term

Support During Labor

Combining relaxation and breathing techniques may help hasten the birth process and can help you cope with the discomfort of the contractions. Remember, though, these techniques are only tools. As much as we wish they could, they cannot decrease the pain of childbirth.

Relaxation Techniques

Relaxation should be one of your ongoing goals during labor and birth. When you focus on relaxing your body, you help your muscles do their work during labor and the birth of your baby.

- *Total body relaxation*: This involves allowing all your muscles to become limp so your body feels like a rag doll.

- *Progressive relaxation*: This technique involves tensing and releasing different muscle groups, starting with your facial muscles and moving down to your feet.

- *Touch relaxation*: The purpose for this is to consciously relax specific muscles by lightly massaging them. If for some reason it makes you uncomfortable to be touched, this tool may not help you relax.

- *Effleurage*: The laboring mother usually does this. Consciously relax your abdominal and perineal muscles by gently stroking your abdomen.

- *Showering*: Warm water from the shower massages your body, helping it relax.

• *Changing position*: This can relax the body by integrating the contracting uterus into other body movements, such as rocking in a chair, doing the pelvic rock, or even squatting.

Breathing Techniques

There are several ways that breathing techniques can help while you're in labor. Like relaxation techniques, they are tools that can help you cope with the discomfort of contractions.

In Early Labor

• *Deep, relaxed, cleansing breaths*:
Before and after each contraction, take a deep, relaxed breath to ensure a proper balance of oxygen and carbon dioxide. Breathe in through your nose and exhale completely through your mouth. Placing your tongue behind your front teeth during each breathing pattern will help keep your mouth from becoming dry.

• *Slow, relaxed chest breathing*:
Breathe in through your nose and out through your mouth in a controlled, slow, relaxed manner. Breathe deeply and slowly at a rate of eight to ten breaths per minute.

As Labor Intensifies

• *Accelerated chest breathing*:
Increase your rate of breathing as the intensity of the contraction increases. Decrease your breathing rate as the contraction subsides.

- *Patterned chest, or "Hee-Hee-Hee-Hoo," breathing:*
  Each breath consists of three short intakes of air, followed by short exhalations while you say "hee," followed by a longer exhalation while you say "hoo." Each peak on Figure 5.2 represents a separate "hee" or "hoo." For a variation, alternate the number of short breaths. Your labor coach can raise his fingers to indicate the number of "hee" breaths per cycle.

Hee-Hee-Hee-Hoo Breathing

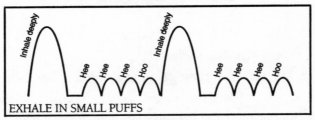

Figure 5.2

During Pushing

- *Slow, controlled exhalation:*
  Inhale quickly, and then exhale slowly while pushing. If another breath is required, repeat the process. Do not hold your breath with this technique.

- *Short breath-holding:*
  Inhale quickly and hold your breath for a count of ten while actively pushing; then release. Repeat until the contraction is over. Your coach can help you by counting out loud during the breath-holding phase.

By providing for an adequate oxygen intake, these breathing techniques also decrease the possibility of hyperventilation (an improper balance of carbon dioxide and oxygen in the blood caused by accelerated breathing). The symptoms of hyperventilation include a very rapid rate of breathing, tingling in hands and feet or around the mouth, dizziness, and numbness of fingers, toes, lips, or tongue. If hyperventilation occurs, notify your doctor, breathe into a bag or cupped hands, and consciously attempt to decrease your rate of breathing until the symptoms subside.

Alternative Positions for Relief of Discomfort During Labor

Rhythmic movements during labor can comfort you, while changing your position can ease your discomfort.

Back Pain and Hard-to-Tolerate Uterine Contractions

• Hands-and-knees position

• Squatting

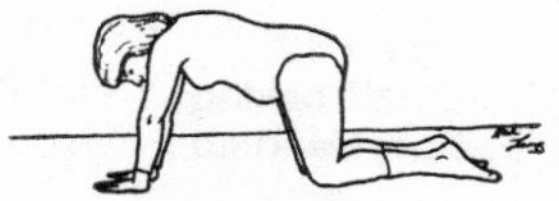

Figure 5.3
Hands-and-Knees

• Standing-rocking position, bending

• Forward lean

• Pelvic rock exercise (see Figure 4.4a on page 57)

Figure 5.4
Forward Lean

Figure 5.5
Variation of Forward Lean

Presence of Fetal Distress

- Hands-and-knees position

- Side-lying position on left side

**Figure 5.6
Squatting**

Slow Progression of Labor

- Hands-and-knees position

- Squatting

- Standing-rocking position, bending

- Sitting in a rocking chair

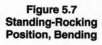

**Figure 5.7
Standing-Rocking
Position, Bending**

- Pelvic rock exercise

Incorrect Position of Baby's Head

- Hands-and-knees position with pelvic rock exercise

- Squatting

- Side-lying position

**Figure 5.8
Side-Lying**

Slow Progression in the Descent of the Baby

- Standing

- Squatting

- Sitting

Alternative Positions for Pushing

Semi-sitting

Used with early pushing to encourage the pre-senting part of the baby to maneuver under the pubic bone.

Figure 5.9
Semi-Sitting

Side-lying

Used for fifteen minutes on each side to encourage the presenting part of the baby to maneuver within the pelvis, especially if the baby's head position is posterior.

Figure 5.10
Side-Lying

Squatting

This position encourages the presenting part of the baby to continue to move down the birth canal and stretches the perineum by applying gentle pressure to it. It's best to use this at the end of the pushing stage because if it's started too early or continued for too long, the perineum may become swollen. For support, use a squat bar, hold on to the side of the bed or a desk, or straddle a door while holding on to both doorknobs.

PURE

PURE is an acronym that stands for a combination of steps you can take to relax and help alleviate discomfort and pain during labor. It helps you remember four things:

- **P**osition (change frequently)

Figure 5.11
Squatting

- **Urination** (empty bladder frequently)
- **Relaxation** (use relaxation techniques)
- **Environment** (change lighting, add music, decrease outside noise)

The Stages of Labor

During labor, your cervix effaces (thins) and dilates (stretches and expands), and your uterus contracts. Together, these processes allow the baby to pass through the cervix and push him down the birth canal and into the world. Labor is divided into three distinct stages, each of which has a specific purpose and specific characteristics.

First Stage of Labor: Early Phase

Dilation: Zero to four centimeters

Effacement: varies by individual
(usually 20 to 50 percent)

Characteristics:

**Figure 5.12
Beginning Labor**

- Contractions last from thirty to forty-five seconds and occur every five to twenty minutes.

- Blood-tinged mucous (show) is discharged from the vagina.

- Membranes may rupture.

**Figure 5.13
60 percent
effacement
0 to 1 cm dilated**

- The average time for completion of this stage is eight to twelve hours for a first-time mother and six to eight hours for a mother who has given birth before. This phase is 50 to 60 percent of the entire labor.

First Stage of Labor: Active Phase

Dilation: four to eight centimeters
Effacement: varies by individual
    (usually 50 to 80 percent)
Characteristics:

**Figure 5.14
80 percent
effacement
4 cm dilated**

- Contractions last forty-five to sixty seconds and occur every two to five minutes.

- There is a heavier amount of show, and it is more blood-tinged due to capillary breakage in the dilating cervix.

- The average time for completion of this stage is six hours for a first-time mother and two to three hours for a mother who has given birth before. This stage is 30 to 40 percent of entire labor.

First Stage of Labor: Transition

Dilation: eight to ten centimeters
Effacement: 100 percent
Characteristics:

**Figure 5.15
100 percent
effacement
10 cm dilated**

- Contractions last sixty to ninety seconds and occur every one to three minutes.

• There is heavy show with an increased amount of blood.

• The average time for completion of this stage is thirty minutes to three hours for a first-time mother and fifteen minutes to one hour for a mother who has given birth before. This is the shortest phase of labor.

Second Stage of Labor: Pushing and Birth
Dilation: ten centimeters
Characteristics:

• Contractions last sixty to seventy seconds and occur every three to five minutes.

• The average time for completion of this stage is thirty minutes to two hours for a first-time mother and fifteen minutes to one hour (up to three hours with an epidural) for a mother who has given birth before.

Third Stage of Labor: Separation of Placenta
Characteristics:

• Contractions may occur closer together but be less painful.

• Lasts anywhere from a few minutes to an hour.

The flow chart at the end of this chapter summarizes the stages of labor. For more detailed information about the stages of labor, as well as the care of the mother after delivery, see Appendix D, "The Stages of Labor." The tables there describe the physical and emotional symptoms associated with each stage, what you should do and comfort measures you can take during each stage, and how your labor coach can help you.

Emergency Childbirth

We began this chapter with the observation that none of us knows when labor will commence. We've all heard of cases where a woman in labor didn't make it to the hospital in time for the birth of her baby. Since this can happen to anyone, you should prepare yourself by learning what to do in case it happens to you or someone you are with. If you see that the woman is about to give birth, here's what to do:

• Stay calm.

• Call 911 for assistance.

• Help the mother to a comfortable position (reclining on a bed, on the seat of the car, or on the floor).

• Gather clean towels and blankets (they don't need to be sterile).

• Keep the mother warm.

• Wash your hands thoroughly (if possible).

- When you can see the top of the baby's head bulging on the perineum, encourage the mother to use candle-blow breathing while you support the baby's emerging head with your cupped hand.

- Wipe the baby's nose and mouth free of mucous and fluid with a clean cloth.

- Carefully feel around the baby's neck for the umbilical cord. If the cord is around the neck, gently slip it over the baby's head. *Do not* pull on or cut the umbilical cord. The placenta will deliver itself, usually within ten minutes. A gush of blood may signal this. Wrap the placenta and keep it close by the baby. Save all the mother's birth products.

- Dry the baby with a clean towel. If he does not begin breathing spontaneously, stimulate him by vigorously rubbing his back. Remove any remaining mucous and fluid from his mouth and nose with a bulb syringe, if available, or a clean cloth. If the baby still doesn't respond, begin mouth-to-mouth resuscitation and cardiopulmonary resuscitation (CPR).[6]

- Immediately after birth, dry the baby, wrap him, place him face down on his mother's abdomen, and cover him with blankets to keep him warm. Allow him to breast-feed as soon as possible to help stimulate contractions of the mother's uterus.

- Massage the mother's abdomen to keep the uterus contracting. The uterus should feel like a grapefruit at the level of the navel.

- Clean the mother's perineum by wiping away from the vaginal opening toward the rectum. If a clean sanitary pad is available, place it over the perineum.

- Take the mother, baby, and birth products to the hospital for evaluation.

Labor Flowchart

First Stage
Beginning of labor
    Contractions are five to twenty minutes apart
    Duration of contractions is thirty to forty-five seconds
    ▼

    Change in activity . . . . Cessation of contractions or
        decrease in intensity or regularity
        (false labor Braxton-Hicks
        contractions)

    ▼
    Intensity remains the same or increases
    Intervals are regular or closer together
    Duration is the same or longer, up to approximately one-and-a-half minutes

Early labor (smiling phase)
Zero to four centimeters
    Continue normal activities as long as possible
    Walk
    Maintain normal breathing patterns . . .▶ Slow, relaxed chest breathing
    Drink clear liquids
    Take a shower or bath if membranes have not ruptured
    Call your coach
    ▼
    Call doctor if:
    ➤ Contractions are five to ten minutes apart
    ➤ Duration of contractions is forty-five to sixty seconds
    ➤ Water breaks
    ➤ Bleeding from the vagina is more than bloody show
    ▼
    Go to the hospital when contractions get more uncomfortable
    (Don't forget the suitcases!)

Admitted if entering active phase . . . . ▶ Go home ▶ Walk, relax, shower
▼ ▼
Vital signs . . . . ◀ Return to the hospital if contractions
increase in intensity or become
▼ more frequent or longer in duration.
Labor information
External monitor . . . . ▶ May be removed after fetal well-
▼ being is established, followed by
Vaginal exam intermittent monitoring if okay with
Blood and urine samples taken doctor (approximately one hour).
IV (as condition indicates)
Enema (as condition indicates)

Active labor (grimace phase 😖)
Four to eight centimeters
Contractions are two to five minutes apart
Duration is forty-five to sixty seconds
▼
Contractions require concentration . . ▶ Slow chest breathing with cleansing
breath before and after each contraction.
Keep room quiet; try to reduce
distractions
Nausea/vomiting . . . . ▶ May need medication if prolonged
and IV fluids to avoid dehydration
Tense/restless . . . . ▶ Walk, shower, change position, have
a back rub, remember PURE. Pain
medication may be used to aid in
relaxation.

Hard labor (shortest phase; birth is near)
Ten centimeters . . . . ▶ Have a support person in constant
attendance. Encouragement, support,
Contractions come two to three and control are needed most at this
minutes apart and peak immediately point. Continue the breathing pattern
Duration is sixty to ninety seconds and movements that have worked
during active stage.
▼
Nausea/vomiting . . . . ▶ May need medication if prolonged
and IV fluids to avoid dehydration
Back pain . . . . ▶ Try hands-and-knees position,
counterpressure, pelvic rock
Leg cramps . . . . ▶ Try position change
Flushed face . . . . ▶ Cool face cloth

Perspiring . . . . ▶ Cool face cloth
Restless/irritable . . . . ▶ Change position, have a back rub,
change environment
Urge to push . . . . ▶ Call for doctor; candle blow until
instructed otherwise

Second stage (pushing, expulsion, birth)
Ten centimeters to birth of baby
Contractions are two to five minutes apart.
Duration is forty-five to ninety seconds.
▼
Irresistible urge to push . . . . ▶ Alert doctor; advance to pushing
▼
Rest between contractions . . . . ▶ Avoid holding breath for long
periods; push at peak of contraction
to a count of ten; release and repeat
throughout contraction; change
pushing positions if needed.

▼
Backache may decrease.
▼
Perineum may have painful
splitting, burning sensation.
▼
Episiotomy may be performed.
▼
Stop pushing as instructed . . . . ▶ Candle blow or pant.

The baby is born!

Third stage (delivery of the placenta)
Many times unnoticed by mother
Contractions cease with birth of baby and then resume until placenta is delivered
▼
Put baby to breast (if it is possible and the mother wants to)
▼
Placenta is delivered
▼
Examination for tears and/or repair of episiotomy
▼
Begin postpartum care

Chapter Six

Birth by Cesarean Section

*D*uring the delivery of Annette's first child, Pitocin was being administered after many hours of labor to help strengthen her contractions—when suddenly the baby showed signs of acute fetal distress. Her doctor told her that an immediate C-section was necessary to save the baby's life. Despite a flurry of emotions, Annette had peace. She and her husband had spent a lot of time preparing for this possibility, and now here it was.

Annette's husband, who was able to witness the birth, felt a sense of helplessness when the baby arrived purple and lifeless, but that quickly changed to amazement and thankfulness when their little boy immediately "pinked up" in response to resuscitation measures. In the following days, as her husband and her doctor described the tense moments in the operating room, Annette found herself in tears at the thought of what could have happened had the nurses and doctors not reacted so swiftly.

As was the case with Annette, there are situations in which a Cesarean Section may become necessary. In this chapter we tell you a little about the history of C-sections, describe the conditions that may make one essential, and then tell you what you can expect if you have one.

A Short History of Cesarean Section

A Cesarean Section is a surgery in which an incision is made through the abdomen and into the uterus to remove the baby. This kind of surgery has been around a long time. There are references to it in ancient Hindu, Egyptian, Greek, Roman, and European folklore. How it got its name is shrouded in myth. It is commonly attributed to the surgical birth of Julius Caesar, but that is highly unlikely. A more likely explanation is that under Caesar, Roman law decreed that all women who wouldn't survive the birth of their child must be cut open—hence the term *cesarean*. Another possibility is that the term comes from the Latin word *caedare*, which means "to cut." Although it's hard to pinpoint the origin of the procedure or its name, we do know that it was done as a last resort to save the life of the baby, not the mother. It wasn't until the nineteenth century that it became possible to use it to save both mother and child.

With the discovery of anesthesia and an increase in the number of hospitals after the mid-nineteenth century, C-sections became a common procedure. In the twentieth century the procedure became increasingly elective, and in the second half of the century the rate of C-sections increased from 5 percent to 25 percent of all deliveries. The wisdom of the day was "once a Cesarean Section, always a Cesarean Section."

By the early 1980s, however, women were viewing the birth experience more positively, and they began to see C-sections as unnecessary surgery. As a result, groups organized to encourage "vaginal birth after Cesarean Section," or VBAC. By the end of the decade the number of C-sections began to level off, while the VBAC rate increased. Today the pendulum has begun to swing back to "once a C-section, always a C-section," largely because of the risks associated with VBACs and the rising rate of malpractice suits.[7]

A previous Cesarean Section is the most common indicator of delivery by C-section. However, there are many other reasons for having one, and it's important for you to be familiar with them so you can take steps to avoid one if possible. (This information is summarized in Appendix E, "Cesarean Section.")

Conditions Indicating the Need for a C-Section

Difficult Labor

Cephalopelvic Disproportion (CPD)

This term simply means that the size of the baby does not match the size of the birth canal. There are many reasons for this.

Obviously, a very large baby won't have an easy time getting through a small pelvis. It would

**Cephalopelvic
Disproportion**

be nice to be able to know that this is going to be a problem, but unfortunately there's no way to tell exactly how big your baby will be. Your doctor can get a rough idea by feeling your abdomen, and an ultrasound might help him make an estimate, but the results of both methods can be off by 15 percent, which can mean that a baby estimated to weigh ten pounds can actually weigh anywhere between eight and a half and eleven pounds. In addition, an abnormal pelvis cannot readily be diagnosed with a pelvic examination unless it is excessively small or the woman has had a pelvic fracture.

It isn't possible to predict what size baby can pass through a given pelvis. The fact that any sizable baby can pass through such a small opening is a miracle in itself. The external size of the pelvis is not necessarily an indication of the internal size of the pelvis, and in fact, very petite women can deliver very big babies. The fact that labor is a dynamic process is another factor. The ligaments that hold the pelvic bones together may stretch some in pregnancy, enlarging the pelvis. Also, the bones of the baby's head are not fused yet, so during birth a large head may mold to fit the pelvis.

There are some risks associated with delivering a large baby vaginally, and these may be of concern to your doctor. These can include vaginal tears and injuries to your baby such as fractured bones and permanent nerve damage. Severe cases can lead to permanent brain damage in the baby, or even death.

Abnormal Contractions

Irregular, weak, or uncoordinated contractions can slow the process of labor. Early labor (dilation up to four centimeters) is considered abnormal if it lasts longer than twenty hours in a first pregnancy or fourteen hours in a subsequent one. If you are exhausted, but there is no indication of fetal distress, your doctor may consider inducing labor by using Oxytocin (a synthetic replica of a natural chemical in the woman's body) to improve the strength and frequency of your contractions.

Many women fear that Oxytocin will increase their pain or harm the baby. Oxytocin will increase the pain, but that's the idea. Without it, the contractions aren't strong enough to be effective. The pain is generally no greater than if labor were proceeding normally. There is a risk of fetal distress if too much Oxytocin is given too quickly. That's why it is begun at a very low dose and increased gradually. The baby is also carefully monitored, and if there are signs of fetal distress, the infusion of Oxytocin is discontinued. An alternative is nipple stimulation, which releases Oxytocin naturally, but the contractions produced are usually not as strong or as effective.

Abnormal Presentation of the Baby

Occiput Posterior

The occiput is the top of the back of the baby's head, where the diameter of the head is the smallest. Normally during birth, this is the part that presents itself first, so that the baby's face is towards the mother's back. If there is a change in this position and the baby is face up (*occiput posterior*), the presenting part of the head will have a greater diameter, making for a much more difficult delivery.

There is no way for your doctor to rotate the baby's head during labor. If it is suspected that your baby's head position is abnormal, you can try changing positions to get his head to rotate. This is particularly important if you have been laboring mainly on your back. Assuming a knee-chest position may be helpful. Sometimes just waiting for rotation to occur naturally works. Epidural anesthesia can hinder the rotation of the baby's head.

Breech

The most common abnormal presentation is breech, or when the feet or buttocks present first. Your doctor can diagnose this before labor begins by palpating your abdomen to locate the baby's head and back, and sometimes through a vaginal examination.

Breech Position Once it is diagnosed, the baby's position is confirmed by ultrasound.

Most of the time, a baby will be in a head-down position by week thirty-six or thirty-seven. It is unlikely that he will turn after that time.

If the baby is breech after the thirty-sixth week, your doctor will want to talk with you about your birth options. There are many risks associated with delivering a breech baby vaginally, and for that reason most doctors do not perform them. In fact, it may be hard to find a doctor with experience in vaginal breech deliveries. If you are seriously considering this option, you may want to deliver at a university hospital with a perinatologist in attendance.

At times a cesarean section can be avoided through what is called an "external cephalic version." In this procedure, medication is introduced through an IV line to relax the uterus and allow it to be manipulated. With the guidance of ultrasound, external manual pressure is applied to move the baby. The chance of success is greatest when the baby is not extremely large and there is adequate fluid around him. It's also easier to turn the baby if it is your second or third pregnancy. The abdominal wall is more relaxed, which allows for easier manipulation. If the external version is successful, your doctor may want to induce labor immediately to ensure that the baby does not turn back to the breech position.

Fetal Distress

This can occur before or during labor. If there are concerns about the health of your baby during labor, you will have continuous fetal heart-rate monitoring, using either an external monitor or a scalp electrode if needed. A scalp electrode provides a more accurate reading of the baby's heart rate. It doesn't cause the baby any discomfort, and complications from it are very rare. Your doctor is looking for a decrease in the baby's heart rate or any other indications of fetal distress. If there are concerns, you will be turned on your side and given oxygen. You may be examined vaginally to check for a prolapsed cord. If you are on oxytocin, it will be discontinued. If the heart rate continues to be abnormal, you may have to have an emergency C-section.

Problems With the Placenta

Placenta previa and placental abruption (discussed in chapter 8) are other indicators of the need for cesarean section. If there is evidence of hemorrhaging, an emergency C-section will be performed. In the case of placental abruption, if labor is progressing rapidly and there is no evidence of fetal distress, a **Prolapsed Cord** vaginal birth may be possible.

What to Expect if You Have a C-Section

Before Surgery

Before a C-section you will be asked to sign a consent form for the surgical procedure. Blood will be drawn for a blood count and evaluation of blood type, and a urine specimen will be sent for analysis. Your abdomen and pubic area may be shaved. An IV will be started, and a catheter will be inserted into the bladder. **Placenta Previa** der. The IV is necessary to administer anesthetics, analgesics (pain reducers), and antiemetics (antivomiting and anti-nausea medications). Catheterization is a standard procedure for all pelvic surgeries, as it drains the urine, allowing an empty bladder during the procedure. (The bladder is close to the uterus.)

The catheter will be removed between six to twenty-four hours after surgery. Large amounts of fluids will be given before, during, and after the procedure through the IV line, which will usually be removed the next morning, once an adequate intake of oral fluids is established and as soon as there is an adequate urine output.

During Surgery

You will be taken on a gurney into a standard operating room and placed on your back on the surgical table with your arms extended from your sides. Your arms and legs may be strapped to the table. You will be completely covered with sterile drapes, with only the operative site exposed. Oxygen will be administered through a mask or small tubing placed at the openings of your nose.

A number of people may be present during surgery, including the obstetrician, surgical assistant, scrub nurse, circulating nurse, anesthesiologist, nursery nurse, pediatrician, and respiratory therapist. Except in cases of extreme emergency, or when a general anesthesia is being used, the father is usually allowed in the operating room after the anesthesia is administered.

The types of anesthesia commonly used for cesarean deliveries are general, epidural, or spinal (see "Anesthesia Used for Labor and Delivery" in Appendix C). To control postoperative pain, morphine may be administered at the same time as a spinal, or at the end of the procedure with an epidural.

The procedure itself is normally performed using a horizontal or bikini-cut incision along the pubic hairline. A vertical incision is not common except in cases of extreme emergency. When spinal or epidural anesthesia is used, you can feel tugging and pressure, especially during the removal of the baby. The surgical assistant or the scrub nurse will press on the upper abdomen to assist in removing the baby, and once the baby is out, these sensations decrease. It's important to tell the anesthesiologist if these sensations are painful, as medications can be given to relieve your discomfort.

The baby's vital signs (breathing, heart rate, and temperature) will be immediately monitored and evaluated by a nurse or pediatrician. If the C-section was performed because of difficulties with the baby, he may be moved to the hospital nursery or neonatal intensive care unit (NICU) for further evaluation and treatment. If there are no complications, the father may be allowed to hold the baby during the completion of the procedure, which takes from thirty to sixty minutes.

After the surgical procedure is completed, you will be taken to the recovery room for one to two hours. The nurses will monitor your vital signs, evaluate vaginal bleeding, observe the abdominal dressing, and palpate the top of your uterus every fifteen minutes. Oxygen may be administered during the early part of recovery. During this time you may experience pain, nausea, vomiting, or cramping. Tell the nurse about any discomfort you have so she can give you medication to minimize it.

When an epidural anesthesia has been used, your ability to move will return before sensation does. You should regain muscle control within the first few hours after the C-section. When a spinal anesthesia has been used, movement and sensation return within one to four hours after surgery.

After Surgery

Within the first eight to twenty-four hours after surgery, you'll be helped out of bed and encouraged to walk. Walking helps return bowel activity to normal and aids in the elimination of postoperative intestinal gas, which can cause you some discomfort. Besides walking, remedies include taking antigas medications and analgesics as prescribed. Frequent coughing and deep breathing is also encouraged to help prevent pneumonia. You can shower after the abdominal dressing is removed, usually within twelve to twenty-four hours after surgery.

When you breathe, you may experience pain in the shoulder area. This is due to the accumulation of free air in the abdomen that settles under the diaphragm. Remedies include lying on the side that hurts (with the head of the bed in a flat position), drinking warm fluids, and using a heating pad. Laxatives or enemas may also be given. This problem is usually resolved within twenty-four to forty-eight hours.

Your diet will progress from clear liquids to regular food as tolerated. Large quantities of fluids and a high-fiber diet are encouraged. Medications for pain, nausea, and constipation are available as approved by your doctor.

Most patients are discharged from the hospital three to four days after surgery, depending on recovery, caregiver preference, and insurance limits. Pain medications will usually be prescribed for use at home for approximately two weeks.

At Home

The most important thing to remember is that you have just had major surgery. Arrange for help with housework for as long as possible (a recommended minimum is two weeks), and don't lift anything heavier than the baby in the first six to eight weeks after delivery. Get your doctor's approval before you attempt any heavy or strenuous housework. Also get his okay before starting or resuming an exercise regimen. If an activity causes pain, stop; if you're tired, rest. Sleep when the baby sleeps. You should keep trips short, and someone else should drive for at least the first two to three weeks after surgery. It's recommended that you not resume marital relations for four to six weeks. Be sure to notify your doctor if you experience heavy bleeding, increased abdominal pain, fever, or drainage from the incision.

Most women naturally want to give birth to a child without surgery, and those who have to have a cesarean when they planned to deliver vaginally can experience some strong emotions. Many women consider the use of forceps, vacuum extractors, and cesarean section extreme, artificial measures for delivery. Nevertheless, to achieve a healthy outcome, you need to remain flexible.

If you're worried that you may need to have a C-section, you should learn everything you can and then discuss your concerns with your doctor, especially with regard to when he would consider surgical intervention. A cesarean section may become necessary. If it does, you'll be prepared.

Chapter Seven

Why Us?

We wish a chapter like this was not necessary. We wish every pregnancy could follow a divine play book where all outcomes are predictably wonderful. Unfortunately the human condition does not allow that type of perfection, and a chapter like this is necessary because sometimes the outcome of a pregnancy is very different from what you planned, expected, or wanted. Your labor may begin prematurely, you may have more babies than you're ready for, you might miscarry, or your baby might be stillborn or born with abnormalities. Probably the most common question asked by parents facing undesired outcomes is "Why us?"

This chapter provides information that will help you know if you are at risk for some of these outcomes and, if so, some things that might help prevent them. This information will also help you understand in most cases, what can cause a deviation from the norm. However, it's also important to realize that you may never know if something goes wrong, exactly why it happened—or why it happened to you.

Preterm Delivery

In the United States, 10 to 11 percent of all births occur before the thirty-seventh week of pregnancy. In approximately 30 percent of these cases, either the mother or her baby has complications that make an early delivery necessary. In the other 70 percent, preterm labor occurs spontaneously. Often the cause can be identified, but not the reason for it. In such cases, medical treatment and a temporary change in the mother's lifestyle may postpone delivery.

Indications That Delivery Will be Preterm

Pregnancy-induced Hypertension (PIH, or Preeclampsia)

PIH is a condition that manifests itself as elevated blood pressure; protein in the urine; changes in vision; persistent headaches or pain in the upper abdomen; swelling (edema) of the face, hands, and feet; and fluid retention that can lead to rapid weight gain. It occurs more frequently in first pregnancies.

If left untreated, this condition can become severe (eclampsia) and life threatening for both the mother and the child. Complications of PIH include seizures, cerebral (brain) hemorrhage, blindness, kidney failure, coma, and death.

No one knows what causes preeclampsia, and the only cure is delivery. If the case is mild, bedrest (possibly in the hospital) may delay delivery. Worsening of the condition would indicate delivery.

Problems With the Placenta

• *Placenta Previa*

When the placenta is abnormally implanted in the lower segment of the uterus, it can either partially or completely cover the opening of the birth canal. With the expansion of the uterus in the second and third trimester, or with uterine contractions, portions of the placenta may become dislodged and begin to bleed, threatening the lives of both mother and child. In cases of mild vaginal bleeding, bedrest in the hospital or treatment for possible preterm labor may delay delivery.

- *Placental Abruption*

This occurs when a normally implanted placenta separates prematurely from the uterine wall. Though the separated placenta may conceal the bleeding, you may experience abdominal discomfort ranging from mild cramping to severe pain. If the outside borders of the placenta separate, vaginal bleeding may occur along with frequent painful contractions. If bleeding occurs, a C-section will be performed immediately. In severe cases, the fetal mortality rate is high due to an inadequate blood supply to the baby.

Fetal Growth Retardation

This condition is usually diagnosed when it is suspected that the baby is not growing as he should and ultrasound is used to accurately measure him. A number of conditions, both in the mother and the baby, have been associated with abnormal growth. Maternal conditions include hypertension, kidney or lung disease, diabetes, heart disease, lupus, smoking, drug or alcohol use, malnutrition, infections, and exposure to toxins. Fetal chromosomal abnormalities, certain fetal infections (such as rubella), and problems with the placenta can also retard growth.

Mild growth retardation may be managed with bedrest, which helps increase the blood flow to the uterus (if the placenta is normal, regular physical activity does not cause fetal growth retardation). In severe cases, delivery may be recommended because the baby may be able to grow better outside the mother's body. Complications of severe growth retardation can include fetal distress or death.

Conditions Associated With Preterm Delivery

Premature Rupture of Membranes

In approximately 5 to 10 percent of all labors, the amniotic membranes rupture before the onset of labor. A rupture before the thirty-fourth week of gestation may necessitate the delivery of a premature infant. This is seen more frequently in mothers with a multiple pregnancy, a urinary tract or vaginal infection, polyhydramnios (excessive amniotic fluid), or an infection of the amniotic fluid. A premature rupture may occur in women with an incompetent cervix if the membranes protrude through the dilated cervix.

If there is no evidence of a uterine infection, bedrest and observation may manage preterm rupture of the membranes, and this may be recommended if the baby is very premature. However, most women will go into labor within one week of the rupture.

Incompetent Cervix

In this case, the cervix dilates in the second trimester of pregnancy (between about sixteen and twenty-two weeks), causing either a miscarriage or premature delivery. This can occur without the mother even being aware of it. The condition can be the result of a previous surgical procedure to the cervix; damage to the cervix in a previous delivery or abortion; or exposure to diethylstilbestrol (DES), a potent estrogen that can cause birth defects. Many times an incompetent cervix can be managed by a surgical procedure called cerclage, in which one or more sutures are put around the cervix to keep it closed, usually at the beginning of the second trimester. The sutures are removed prior to normal labor and delivery. When done as an elective procedure before any dilation occurs, the procedure has an 85 percent success rate.

Many women with this condition have no risk factors, so it's often impossible to know that there is an incompetent cervix until it's already dilated. This can happen rapidly with no warning, as the signs may be subtle. If you have increased vaginal discharge (particularly mucus tinged with blood) and unusual low back pain, you should contact your doctor.

Abnormalities in the Uterus

These may include an abnormally shaped uterus or a uterus in which fibroids (noncancerous growths that form in the internal uterine wall) are present.

Infection

Bacterial infections can release toxins that stimulate the uterus and perhaps bring on premature labor.

Other Conditions

A number of other factors have been linked to preterm labor:

- *Polyhydramnios*
  This is a condition marked by an excessive amount of amniotic fluid, which in turn may be the result of abnormalities in the baby (such as fetal malformation or obstruction of the digestive or urinary tract),

a multiple pregnancy, or maternal conditions (such as preeclampsia and diabetes).

• *Previous Abortions*
Recent studies indicate that a woman who has had two or more abortions (especially in the second trimester of pregnancy) has a higher risk of premature birth. This also applies to women who have had two or more miscarriages. The exact reason is not known.

• *Maternal Conditions*
Women who have certain medical conditions during pregnancy have a higher incidence of preterm delivery. These include cardiac or renal disease, high blood pressure, Diabetes, and Sickle-Cell Anemia.

• *Drugs, Alcohol, and Smoking*
Smoking cigarettes, drinking large amounts of alcohol, and using drugs (such as cocaine and heroin), can result in both preterm labor and low birth weight.

• *Inadequate Prenatal Medical Care*
This is associated with preterm labor because it doesn't allow a doctor to monitor the mother's nutritional intake or to provide an early diagnosis of potential complications.

• *Age of the Mother*
Mothers under the age of seventeen and over the age of thirty-five have more premature deliveries than women in other age-groups. This is possibly due to an older woman's increased incidence of com-

plications during her pregnancy and to a younger woman's need for a higher nutritional intake to provide for her own development as well as the baby's.

• *Emotional Stress*
Several studies have shown that maternal stress is associated with preterm birth. Ambivalent feelings toward the pregnancy or the baby itself, however, have not been shown to increase the chance of premature delivery.

Even though a premature infant may require intensive medical intervention at the beginning, you need to be involved in the care of your baby. This may mean no more than your gentle touch on his hand. You have a vital role to play in your baby's life, and that doesn't change because he is premature or sick. The child needs you to provide what the medical profession cannot—a parent's love and tenderness.

More Than One Baby

The incidence of twin pregnancies is approximately one in 85 births for Caucasians, one in 50 for African Americans, and one in 150 for Asians. Births of more than two infants at the same time are not as common, but the incidence of higher multiples in pregnancy is increasing because of medical procedures that stimulate the ovaries, In Vitro Fertilization, and embryo transfers.

The most common complications of a multiple pregnancy are preterm labor and preeclampsia. The incidence of preeclampsia is up to three times higher for a multiple than a single birth, and preterm labor is ten times more common. More than one-half of multiple births are delivered prematurely, and preterm birth is the leading cause of neonatal death in multiple gestations.

Difficulties with the placenta (placental abruption and placenta previa), polyhydramnios, gestational Diabetes (Diabetes that occurs only during pregnancy), and premature rupture of membranes are also more common in multiple births. Babies of multiple pregnancies are often smaller than average for their gestational age, which may be due to problems with the placenta or nutritional intake that doesn't provide them with what they need to grow at the normal rate.

If you are carrying more than one baby, you'll need closer supervision, more rest, and an extra-nutritional diet. Multiple babies are usually delivered by Cesarean Section, which can cause some people concern. Financial concerns also increase as the number of babies increases.

Miscarriage

A miscarriage (also called a spontaneous abortion) is the delivery of a baby before he can survive outside the womb. It is estimated that approximately 20 percent of all pregnancies result in miscarriages. The actual number may be higher because a large number of miscarriages are undetected or unreported. Three-fourths of all miscarriages occur within the first twelve weeks of gestation.

Kinds of Miscarriages
- In a *threatened abortion*, a woman experiences discomfort and vaginal bleeding, yet her cervix remains completely closed. One-half of all women who experience vaginal bleeding in the first trimester complete their pregnancies.

- A *missed abortion* is one in which the baby dies or never develops in the uterus, but the baby is not expelled. The cervix remains closed, although some vaginal spotting may occur. When there is no identifiable fetus in the amniotic sac, the condition is known as a "blighted ovum."

- In an *inevitable abortion*, a woman's cervix is dilated, and she experiences pain and heavier vaginal bleeding. In this case, the process of miscarriage has progressed to the point that it is impossible to maintain a viable pregnancy.

- In an *incomplete abortion* the products of conception are not completely expelled from the uterus, while in a *complete abortion* they are.

- *Habitual abortion* refers to an abortion occurring in a woman who has had three or more consecutive spontaneous abortions.

Causes of Miscarriage

Incorrect Development of the Baby

This is primarily the result of chromosomal defects, which account for approximately one-half of all spontaneous abortions. The earlier the miscarriage is in the pregnancy, the more likely it is due to a chromosomal defect.

Improper Implantation of the Embryo in the Uterine Wall

This may be due to the fact that there was an IUD in the uterine cavity at the time of conception, a severely inflamed or irritated uterine lining at the time of implantation, or decreased amounts of the hormone progesterone in the mother's bloodstream in the early stages of pregnancy. A lack of progesterone can lead to poor development of the uterine lining and excessive irritability of the uterus, causing a spontaneous expulsion of the fetus.

Malformations of the Uterus

The shape of the uterus, the embryo's position in it, and the presence of fibroids can result in improper implantation of the embryo and miscarriage. An incompetent cervix can also cause spontaneous abortions by failing to keep the fetus in the uterus. This may occur during the second trimester.

Maternal Conditions

Several maternal medical conditions have been associated with miscarriage, including poorly controlled Diabetes, AIDS, infections such as rubella, immune conditions such as Lupus, and inherited blood-clotting disorders. Smoking, drug and alcohol abuse, and excessive consumption of caffeine can also be contributing factors, as can certain toxins or medications and high doses of radiation.

Trauma to the Uterus

This may be the result of direct physical trauma to the uterus or surgical manipulation of the uterus or abdomen. Sexual activity, exercise, a single previous miscarriage, and emotional trauma have not been directly linked to an increase in the number of miscarriages women experience.

In the majority of cases, there is no obvious reason for a miscarriage. You may blame yourself, but there is rarely anything you could do, short of inflicting a major trauma on yourself, that would cause a miscarriage. Even bedrest won't help most of the time because it doesn't address the things that cause a miscarriage to take place. If you have one miscarriage, there's only about a 20 percent chance that you'll have another.

Stillbirth

A stillbirth is the delivery of a baby who weighs over 500 grams and has died in the uterus after the twenty-second week of gestation. This category does not include neonatal death, which is the death of an infant within the first twenty-eight days of life.

Although in up to 50 percent of stillbirths the reason for the baby's death cannot be determined, several factors may contribute:

• premature detachment of the placenta from the uterine wall (placental abruption)

• compression of the umbilical cord during delivery (either by the baby holding and compressing the cord or by the cord's compression between the baby's head and the mother's pelvic structure)

• strangulation by the umbilical cord

• maternal Hypertension, Eclampsia, or Diabetes

• severely stressful or prolonged labor and delivery

• the presence of severe abnormalities in the baby

Malformations and Illnesses

Malformations occur in approximately 3 to 5 percent of all newborn infants. These can range from minor to disfiguring to severe and life threatening. Abnormalities can occur no matter how good the mother's health is or how cautiously she uses medications.

The percentage of children born with abnormalities is very small, but to a parent whose child is not perfect, even a minor malformation (such as a birthmark) can be devastating. You may feel guilty and search for the reason for the defect, even though most of the time there isn't any obvious explanation for it.

Healthy Responses to Unexpected Outcomes

The loss of a baby before birth can cause severe emotional stress, and if you experience this, you will go through the same grieving process as parents whose babies die after birth. Likewise, someone who gives birth to a child who is premature, ill, or born with abnormalities will have emotional reactions similar to those of a person whose child dies.

If your baby dies after birth, you may wish to see the child either directly or in a photograph taken in the nursery or delivery room. This allows you to remember his face instead of emptiness. You may wish to hold him. We encourage this because it can help you adjust to the reality of your situation. You need to make such requests known to doctors and nurses. You have the right to have your desires met at this critical time.

You might also want to have a funeral service for the child and keep special items that will help you remember him as a family member, like his hospital identification tags, a special blanket made for him, or pictures. Knowing that this may be very difficult to do immediately after the loss of your baby, chaplain's offices in many hospitals keep mementos of stillborn or neonatal deaths for a significant period of time. This enables a family who may not initially want to keep these items to get them at a later date.

If you experience an undesired outcome, you'll need to communicate your feelings openly with others who can relate to you and give you the support you need. Grieving tends to occur in stages, and as you work through them, time will help you accept your loss, whatever it may be. The pain of the loss never completely disappears, but as you accept it, it will become integrated into your life and no longer immobilize you in your day-to-day activities. You will be able to renew old activities and relationships and enter into new ones. Many couples find that in helping other couples going through similar experiences, they help themselves as well.

Getting as much information as possible about your loss will help you not blame the outcome on yourself or others. Many excellent organizations provide this kind of support. You can find them with the help of local churches, hospitals, or the American Red Cross.[8]

Physical Adjustment

During a time of grieving, both parents need to get adequate rest and nutrition. The fatigue that accompanies lack of sleep in a time of stress can result in an emotional overload. You may find yourself having uncontrolled crying spells, difficulty sleeping, digestive disturbances, loss of appetite, and an inability to concentrate.

A woman's body has already been through significant changes by the time an unexpected loss like this occurs. When your baby dies, your body doesn't understand that the pregnancy has ended in tragedy, and so it continues getting ready to nourish the infant. It takes approximately six weeks for the body to heal physically and make the adjustments necessary to get back to normal after a pregnancy. Your doctor can give you practical advice about things you can do to make the adjustment easier.

Practical Assistance

Some outcomes may require you to stay in bed for weeks or months. While you will need encouragement on an ongoing basis, you may also need the help of others with the daily activities you would otherwise do yourself. There also may be older children in the family with needs you may not be able to meet. Here are some ways to help make this situation easier:

• Where finances allow, investigate agencies that provide part-time, full-time, or live-in help. This is especially helpful if you cannot be left alone, or if there are older children who need supervision.

• Create a schedule for family members and friends to help with household chores and provide meals and company for you. In some cases, it may be easier for you to stay in another home where constant assistance is available. Take into consideration the need for comfortable, familiar surroundings and the distance to proper medical facilities.

- When other children are involved, try to maintain as normal a lifestyle as possible. It is also important for them to be in familiar surroundings with frequent contact with you. Plan activities that include you while you're on bedrest, such as reading, coloring, doing simple crafts, sorting laundry, and watching videos. These activities will change as your condition does.

- If meals are being provided, make people aware of any food allergies, your favorite foods, and what foods have been provided recently. It's very helpful to have the meals brought in disposable containers.

- If there are special family occasions such as birthdays or anniversaries that need to be shopped for, ask someone to do it for you.

- Have a date night with your husband. Order takeout food and a video, and find a friend who can keep the children at their home for the evening.

- If you're hospitalized, you'll need constant reassurance that things are under control at home. If possible, call home frequently. Have a family member bring pictures and other familiar personal items to the hospital.

The creative possibilities are endless. Flexibility is the key to making a difficult situation easier.

Chapter Eight

Postpartum Challenges

The six-week postpartum period is a special time for your growing family, now that what was once a dream has become reality. But it is also a challenging time as your body returns to normal and you and your husband take on new responsibilities of nurturing a little life totally dependent on you. It's wise to recognize and prepare for the physical and emotional challenges you will face during this period. The last thing you need to add to your postpartum trials is more fatigue, confusion, and discouragement associated with nurturing a newborn and sleepless nights. Therefore, before your baby arrives, please, for your baby's sake and your sanity, pick up and read *On Becoming Babywise*. It will give you confidence and a working knowledge of infant care and management.

Meanwhile, you will want to become aware of the following post-pregnancy related topics.

Physical Changes

There will be a number of physical changes taking place in your body after your baby arrives. Speaking positively about these changes, there are some things you can do to diminish the stress and strain on your body as it begins to work its way back to a pre-conception condition. To help protect your body and emotions, consider how to care for your:

Uterus

Your uterus has just spent nine months expanding to accommodate your growing baby. Now continuous contractions are returning it to normal size by closing down it's blood vessels. Breast-feeding enhances these contractions by stimulating the production of oxytocin. You can use mild pain relievers to reduce the discomfort caused by the cramping, but avoid products that contain aspirin. Remember to rest, and avoid extended periods of activity.

Perineum

If you had an episiotomy, the stitches (sutures) do not need to be removed—the body will absorb them. There also may have been some minor tears that did not require suturing. Some pain and swelling is normal during the healing process, and your doctor may recommend a mild pain reliever.

Applying a cool compress to the perineum will help reduce the swelling and relieve the discomfort. You can freeze wet washcloths in plastic bags for this purpose. A sitz bath is both soothing and cleansing. Sit in the tub and circulate two to three inches of plain warm water around the perineal area. Disinfect the tub between baths. Other measures you can take to relieve discomfort and promote healing include:

• Don't stand for long periods of time.

- Eliminate strain on the perineum by using a doughnut pillow when you sit, and rest on your side, taking the weight off your bottom.
- Do Kegel exercises to help restore your muscle tone.
- Rinse the perineum with warm water after every visit to the bathroom.
- Use Tucks pads and anesthetic spray for comfort as needed.

Vaginal Discharge (lochia)

The uterus will continue to shed its lining for up to six weeks after delivery. You should notice the amount of blood decreasing and changing in color and texture as it fades from bright red with small clots to pink and white. Increased vaginal bleeding or a bright red discharge could mean that you're doing too much and need to decrease your level of activity. If bleeding persists, you need to call your doctor. Meanwhile, here are some restrictions that will help you prevent infections and rashes until the flow of lochia stops:

- Avoid using tampons, douches, or vaginal inserts.
- Avoid using deodorant pads.
- Avoid marital intimacy.
- Avoid tub baths and swimming.

If in doubt, call your doctor for advice.

Hemorrhoids

Hemorrhoids can develop from constipation, from the dilation of blood vessels in the rectal area due to the pressure of the baby, or from the strain of pushing during childbirth. A sudden increase in the volume of blood to the rectal area after delivery may cause the swelling of hemorrhoids already present. You can try over-the-counter preparations specifically for hemorrhoids, but if no relief occurs within three or four days or the pain is severe, you should consult your doctor. You can also:

- Take a warm sitz bath three to four times a day, especially after having a bowel movement.
- Apply cool compresses.
- Use Tucks pads.
- Drink plenty of fluids.
- Increase the amount of fruits and vegetables in your diet.
- Use the stool softeners suggested by your doctor.
- Avoid straining.
- Avoid sitting or standing for long periods of time.

Breasts

The breasts enlarge noticeably as they prepare for lactation and breast-feeding. After delivery, they secrete colostrum for three to five days until your milk comes in.

Abdominal Muscles

Your abdominal muscles will have doubled in length to accommodate your growing baby, and it will take at least six weeks for them to return to normal. Faithfully doing the exercises shown on pages 118-120 will help improve your muscle tone.

Weight and Figure

The average weight gain during pregnancy is between twenty-four and thirty-five pounds. If you gained a moderate amount of weight, you may be back at your prepregnancy weight within weeks after delivery. It isn't a good idea to diet in the first few months after delivery or while you're breastfeeding. Your body needs increased amounts of energy and nutrients to keep up with the sudden demands of healing and lactation.

You may have noticed that as your baby grew during pregnancy, your center of gravity slowly shifted. After the birth, it shifts again. If necessary, adjust your movements to accommodate these changes, gradually increasing your activities and exercise.

If you experience any of the following symptoms, you should report them to your doctor immediately:

- fever (temperature over 100.4 degrees)
- chills
- persistent, unusual pain that is not alleviated by a mild pain reliever
- increase in vaginal bleeding or clots more than four to five days after delivery
- burning pain while urinating
- hot, reddened, painful breasts
- foul-smelling or discolored vaginal discharge

Hormones

During pregnancy, the body produces large amounts of progesterone and estrogen. After the delivery of the placenta, there is a sudden decrease in these levels, which may cause you to experience sweating, dizziness, and heart palpitations. To reduce the effects of this change:

- Reduce stress as much as possible.
- Provide time for frequent naps.
- Maintain a nutritionally-balanced diet.
- Drink large amounts of fluids.

Emotional Ups and Downs

The dramatic changes in levels of estrogen and progesterone, particularly in the first twenty-four to thirty-six hours after delivery, along with a sudden change in your lifestyle may produce emotional instability. Often called the "baby blues," this instability can manifest itself anywhere on a continuum from distress to psychosis.

- *Postpartum blues:* These generally occur within the first few days to two weeks after the birth of your baby. You may tend to feel depressed, tired, weepy, and melancholy. Even if you have prepared yourself for these feelings, it may be difficult for you to think rationally during this period.

- *Postpartum depression:* This doesn't tend to occur until a few weeks following birth. One of the greatest contributors to it is sleep deprivation. If it interferes with caring for your baby; or if you have any thoughts about harming yourself, contact your doctor. You may need medication, professional counseling, or both.

- *Postpartum psychosis:* This includes any behavior that threatens the safety of the mother, the baby, or any other family member. Any unsafe behavior should be immediately reported to your doctor. You may need medication to bring your body back into balance, or you may need professional counseling.

Determining the underlying causes of postpartum depression or psychosis can sometimes be difficult because of the subjective nature of the symptoms. Unless there is clearly a physical cause for the emotional imbalance, try to identify possible sources of anxiety. For the sake of your health and the emotional stability of your family, seek help that provides support for your entire family and gives you the hope that this, too, will pass.

We want you to enjoy your new baby and not fear the postpartum period. Knowledge, planning, and open communication are all tools that can help you move through this time successfully. In Appendix F, "Meeting Postpartum Challenges," is a list of some of the reasons for the emotions you may experience during the postpartum period, along with some practical remedies.

Rest, Diet, and Exercise

Rest is an essential part of recovery from pregnancy and delivery. If you are too active during the first two weeks after delivery, bleeding may increase. Sleep when your baby sleeps, and allow others to help with the housework and meals. Establishing a parent-directed feeding method will also provide you with the time you need to rest and recover.[8]

During the postpartum period, a nutritionally-balanced diet is essential, as it gives you the energy you need to complete the healing process and accomplish day-to-day activities. Keep taking prenatal vitamins for as long as you nurse, as your baby's growth and development depend on the nutrients he gets from your milk. During lactation, you should consume approximately two thousand calories and drink eight, eight-ounce glasses of water daily.

Exercise is important in returning your body to its former condition. You can usually begin to exercise two weeks after an uncomplicated vaginal delivery, or six weeks after a C-section. Be sure to check with your doctor before starting an exercise program, as there may be reasons why you should avoid certain exercises. Start your program simply and gradually. Here are some recommended postpartum exercises (many of the prenatal exercises are also appropriate for the postpartum period). Add a new exercise each day.

Day 1

Lie flat on your back, exhale, and forcibly draw in your abdominal muscles. Hold for a count of ten, and then relax.

Day 1

Day 2

Day 2

Lie flat on your back with your arms extended out at right angles from your body. Without bending at the elbows, slowly lift your arms until your hands touch, then lower your arms to starting position.

Day 3

Lie on your back with your arms at your side. Keeping your feet flat on the floor, flex your knees and lift your hips. Hold for a count of three, and then relax.

Day 3

Day 4

Lie flat on your back with knees bent and feet flat on the floor. Simultaneously lift your head and tilt your pelvis inward as you contract your buttocks.

Day 4

Day 5

Day 5

Lie flat on your back with your legs straight and your arms at your sides. Simultaneously lift your left knee and raise your head slightly. Using your right hand, reach for, but do not touch, your left knee. Repeat for the opposite side.

Day 6

Lie flat on your back with your legs straight and your arms at your sides. One leg at a time, flex your knee, bring your foot toward your buttocks, and then straighten your leg.

Day 6

Day 7

Day 7

Lie flat on your back with your legs straight and your arms at your sides. Lift one leg up as high as it will go, then slowly lower it, using your abdominal muscles. Repeat with the opposite leg.

Day 8

Do the same exercise as on the seventh day, but this time lift both legs at the same time.

Day 9

Day 9

Get down on all fours, leaning on your elbows and

Day 8

knees. Keeping your forearms and lower legs together, hump your back upwards while contracting your buttock muscles and drawing in your stomach muscles.

Day 10

Lie flat on your back with your legs either straight or bent and your hands behind your head. Using your abdominal muscles, slowly sit up, and then lie back down.

Day 10

The Husband-Wife Relationship

The shared experience of childbirth can create a special closeness between a husband and wife. The moments spent together as a family recognizing your baby's similarities to both of you, as well as his uniqueness, are very special. These are the building blocks of creating a family identity—enjoy them!

Re-establishing marital intimacy after the birth of a child is a common concern. A husband and wife tend to have very different responses to the idea. The keys to keeping your husband-wife relationship healthy are to communicate openly, be patient, and keep expectations realistic.

Here are a few explanations of what is happening to your body to keep in mind.

Realize that your body must heal properly to avoid infection and pain during marital intimacy. The uterus sheds its blood-rich lining for about four to six weeks following birth. During that time, it is best to avoid inserting anything in the vagina, including tampons and douches. Most couples feel ready to resume physical intimacy by the time vaginal bleeding and discharge have stopped.

Be aware that the initial soreness from perineal lacerations or an episiotomy comes from the swelling that takes place as the tissues regenerate. Mild pain relievers, topical medications, sitz baths, Kegel exercises, proper cleansing, and a healthy diet all contribute to the healing process. Generally, the soreness diminishes within two to four weeks after delivery. The idea of having your tender perineum touched may be a tough psychological hurdle for you to overcome. This is where patience, open communication, and mutual goal-setting come in.

Also remember that intimacy can be expressed in many ways, including the use of kind words, touching, kissing, and caressing. Although our culture often stresses the importance of intercourse, a foundation of mutual appreciation and affection is the real basis of a satisfying marital relationship. While waiting for your body to heal, make a point of enjoying each other in other ways.

Another consideration is your hormonal level—which remains low during lactation, causing vaginal dryness that may persist as long as you are nursing. When the time comes to resume marital intimacy, use a water-soluble lubricant, (such as KY Jelly) to ease the dryness of the vaginal tissues. Also experiment with alternate positions.

Pregnancy, delivery, and nursing put a great deal of physical stress on a woman's body. Since the probability of a healthy pregnancy is due at least in part to the amount of time between pregnancies, you need to decide what you are going to do about contraception before you resume sexual relations. There are two things that are important to remember. First, ovulation can occur prior to the first menstrual period after delivery, and secondly, breast-feeding is not a method of contraception.

Realistic Expectations and Goals

As you adjust to the practical aspects of expanding your family, there are some specific things you can do to avoid disappointment and frustration during the first few weeks after delivery.

First, be realistic about how much you can achieve during the first week at home. It's unrealistic to expect that you'll be able to clean the house and fix dinner every day. Prepare meals ahead and freeze them. Accept offers of meals from others. Welcome help with household chores as long as it is available. Your priorities in these first few weeks are to physically recover and to allow yourself time to care for and get to know your baby.

Second, sit down as a couple (preferably before the baby arrives) and discuss your individual expectations about the postpartum period. List the basic chores that need to be accomplished (taking out garbage, cooking, shopping, feeding the animals, laundry). List the tasks that can be done by outside help, such as relatives or friends (basic housework, vacuuming, cooking, laundry). Talk about how to get help and how long it will be available.

To set simple goals, use the charts provided in appendix G, "Goal Setting in the Postpartum Period." List one thing you want to try to do daily and another to do at least once during the week. Strive to achieve the goals for the current week. The following week, try to continue to meet the goals of the previous week as well as adding some new goals.

Finally, remember this important parenting principle—your new baby is a welcome member of an already established family, not the center of it. Now is a good time to establish or cement friendships with couples who are like-minded about parenting and have been through this stage of it. They will be a valuable source of wisdom and support as you meet the challenges of the postpartum period.

Chapter Nine

Infant Care

The birth of a baby is an awesome experience. An infant brings joy and blessing to the family. But his arrival can also seem overwhelming to parents who suddenly become aware of the ever-changing needs of this little person. That's why we've written this chapter. It gives you the information you need to feel confident as you care for your baby during his first year of life.

Immediate Care of Your Newborn

Immediately after birth, your health-care providers will take several steps to ensure your baby's well-being. Under normal circumstances, here's what they will do:

- Make sure he gets enough oxygen
  - use a bulb syringe to remove mucus from his breathing passages and
  - administer oxygen if necessary

• Place identical identification tags on his wrist and ankle and on your wrist

• Keep him warm
  – dry him off and place him on your abdomen for skin-to-skin contact
  – wrap him in warm blankets, or
  – place him under a radiant warmer

• Evaluate his overall condition and note any abnormalities
  – calculate his age based on his appearance
  – weigh him
  – measure his length, chest, and head, and
  – record his pulse rate, respiratory rate, and temperature

• Remove the excess umbilical cord and saturate the stump with a drying agent

• Instill erythromycin ointment in his eyes to prevent infection

• Give him an injection of Vitamin K to prevent bleeding by aiding blood clotting

Nurses will also assess your baby at one minute and at five minutes after birth, using an Apgar score to help determine if he is having problems after delivery. (Note: This score does not help to identify long-term problems.) A score of seven-to-ten means that the baby is in good condition, while four-to-six signals that there may be a need for initial respiratory assistance. A score of four or below indicates that the baby needs lifesaving intervention.

Apgar Score

Apgar	0	1	2
Appearance (color)	Blue or pale pink	Pink body, blue extremities	Pink
Pulse (heart rate)	Pulse absent	Pulse below 100/min	Pulse above 100/min
Response to stimulation	No response	Grimace	Lusty cry
Muscle tone	No movement	Some movement	Good movement
Respiration	Absent	Slow, irregular breathing; weak cry	Good strong cry

What a Newborn Looks Like

When your first chance arrives to get a really good look at your baby, here are some of the things you are likely to see as you examine him from head to toe.

Head

Your baby may look top-heavy to you. That's because the head is 25 percent of a newborn's body size. The average circumference is thirteen to fourteen inches.

The head has "soft spots." These are "fontanels," or areas of the skull that aren't joined yet, but rather held together by membranes. The fontanel at the back of the head closes at approximately three months of age; the one on the top of the head closes at approximately eighteen months.

Some babies are born with a full head of hair; others have none. It is common for babies to lose some or all of their hair in the weeks after birth.

You may notice little white bumps resembling pimples on the baby's forehead, nose, and cheeks. These are called "milia"—and they are caused by immature oil glands. *Do not attempt to remove them.* They are normal and will disappear without treatment as the baby's glands begin to function.

Eyes

A baby's eyes are usually dark blue-gray at birth. Permanent eye color becomes evident between six months and a year.

Because his eye muscles are not fully developed, your baby may appear to be cross-eyed, but around six months the eyes will focus together. If that is not the case for your little one, his pediatrician will refer you to an ophthalmologist.

Due to the antibiotics given at birth, you may notice some swelling or discharge from the baby's eyes. Normal tearing should begin in the first two to three weeks of life.

Neck

The baby's neck muscles are weak, and his head will need to be supported at all times.

Breasts

There is a transfer of hormones from the mother to the baby during pregnancy, and this sometimes manifests itself in temporarily enlarged breasts in both male and female newborns. There even may be some secretion of milk in the first two weeks of life.

Abdomen

Mainly because of poor muscle tone, a newborn's tummy is usually round and protruding. Swallowed air can also be a factor. The centerpiece of this round little belly is the stump of the umbilical cord.

Genitalia

The genitals of both genders may be swollen or enlarged, and false menstruation or vaginal spotting may be present in girls. This is a normal, temporary condition.

Skin

"Lanugo," or fine downy hair, covers the skin of some newborns. It is seen more frequently in premature infants and usually disappears a few weeks after delivery.

Dry, scaly skin, sometimes accompanied by peeling, is not uncommon. It's usually seen two to three weeks following delivery or in babies born after their due date.

If your baby is dark skinned, you might see "mongolian spots," purplish discolorations of the skin that look like bruises, on his lower back or buttocks. They disappear after a year.

Extremities

Your infant's arms and legs are disproportionately short for his body. His arms are usually bent and held close to the chest with hands in fists, and his legs are in the same position they were in the uterus. Most babies appear bowlegged.

Nails are soft and pliable and are usually long at birth.

What Newborns Can Do

Sensory

- Vision is not perfect at birth. It's estimated that newborns can see a distance of twelve to fifteen inches.
- Hearing becomes very acute several days after delivery. Loud noises are disturbing to most infants, while soft sounds are soothing.
- Taste and smell are both well-developed at birth. Researchers have found that many babies can differentiate between their mother's milk and another woman's milk.
- Babies are sensitive to heat and cold. Their skin will appear blotchy when they are chilled, and their hands and feet will have a bluish tint. If they are over-dressed a rash may develop.

Breathing

Unlike adults, who on the average breathe fourteen to twenty times a minute, the newborn breathes at a rapid rate—twenty to fifty times per minute. It is also normal for breathing to be irregular and shallow. Some babies are noisy breathers at night. Frequent hiccups are also normal, although disconcerting for Mom, even if she did feel them during pregnancy. When the baby's diaphragm matures, they will disappear.

Reflexes

Reflexes indicate the health of the nervous system. Most of the reflexes present at birth are vital for the newborn's survival. As the baby matures, some reflexes will disappear, while others will change.

The *sucking reflex* is very strong at birth and one that the baby practiced in the uterus. Any stimulation of the baby's lips should elicit a sucking response. When the baby's cheek is stroked, he will turn his head in that direction and start *rooting*. Newborns will suck on their thumbs, fingers, or fists and occasionally may have developed the habit of sucking on their arm while in the womb. The *swallowing reflex* has been present since before birth, as babies swallow and excrete amniotic fluid in the uterus. *Gagging* helps prevent choking, while *coughing* helps rid the air passages of mucus.

If you place your finger inside the palm of your baby's hand, he will *grasp* it tightly. The grasp may be strong enough to allow his upper body to be raised up. When you hold him under the arms and raise him to a standing position, he will make *stepping* motions. While he is lying on his back, notice that his head may be turned to one side, with that arm and leg extended and his other arm and leg flexed. This is called *tonic neck*. When the baby is startled, he will thrust out his arms as if to embrace, and his legs will straighten and stiffen. This is called the startle, or *moro*, reflex.

Basic Newborn Care at Home

Caring for the Umbilical Stump

The cord stump will turn black a few days after birth, falling off one to two weeks later.

Guidelines for Caring for the Cord Stump

- Clean the cord stump with cotton balls and swabs dipped in rubbing alcohol. Saturate a cotton ball with rubbing alcohol, and squeeze the excess over the stump. Use a cotton swab dipped in alcohol to wipe around the base of the stump. Do this with each diaper change. The purpose of the alcohol is to dry the cord stump. It will not hurt your baby.

- Prevent the diaper from covering the cord stump. Fold the front flap of the diaper away from your baby's abdomen to keep the cord stump exposed.

- Until the cord stump falls off, avoid clothing that binds your baby around the waist, and don't immerse him in water for a bath.

- After the stump falls off, continue to clean the umbilical area with cotton swabs and rubbing alcohol for a few days.

- *Never* remove the cord stump yourself; it will fall off naturally. If you have any questions, call your pediatrician.

Call the Pediatrician If—

- There is excessive bleeding from the cord stump around the junction to the skin.

- There is pus-like drainage from the cord junction site.

- There is redness and swelling around the cord junction site. (Note: You might notice an unpleasant odor as the cord stump dries. This is normal, but if a foul odor accompanies any of the above symptoms, an infection may be developing. See your doctor.)

Caring for a Circumcision

Circumcision is the surgical removal of the foreskin of the penis. In recent days, the benefits and risks of this procedure have been the subject of much debate, with both sides citing social and physical reasons for their positions. Ultimately, the parents must decide whether circumcision will be performed on their baby boy.

Guidelines for Circumcision Care

• Do not give your baby a tub bath until the area completely heals (approximately four to seven days).

• Clean the area with soft cloth and water. Do not rub.

• Apply a thick coat of Vaseline over the area of exposed tissue and cover with a gauze square. This protects the area from wetness and bacteria. Replace at each diaper change until the area is healed.

Call the Pediatrician If—

• There is excessive bleeding from the site of the circumcision.

• There is swelling, redness, the presence of pus or drainage, or a foul odor.

Burping

During feeding, it's not uncommon for a baby to swallow air, but if the air is allowed to stay in his digestive system, it can cause gas and cramping (colic). We recommend that you burp your baby after nursing on each breast. If you are bottle-feeding him, he should be burped after every one to two ounces of formula he takes in. There are several ways to burp a baby.

You can place your palm over the baby's stomach, hooking your thumb around his side and wrapping the other fingers of your hand around his chest. Your hand should support his weight. Resting his bottom on your knee may be helpful. Lean him over your supporting

Figure 9.1

hand. If he wiggles or needs more support, you can hold his hands with your supporting hand. Place your other hand into a cupped position and pat his back firmly but gently (fig. 9.1).

Figure 9.2

Or you can place your baby high up on your shoulder so that it puts direct pressure on his stomach. Allow his head and arms to dangle freely over your shoulder. Hold on to one of his legs so he doesn't wiggle out of position. Pat his back firmly (fig. 9.2).

A third way is to sit down and put the baby's legs between your legs and drape him over your thigh. You need to bring your legs together for support and prop up the baby's head in one hand while you pat his back with the other (fig. 9.3).

Figure 9.3

Figure 9.4

Finally, you can cradle the baby in your extended arm with his bottom resting in the hand of the same arm (his head will be resting at the elbow). Wrap one of his arms and legs around your extended arm, making sure he is facing outward. This position allows you to have one hand free at all times (fig. 9.4).

At times, air will become trapped in a baby's intestines. Most babies do not like to expel gas, and they'll resist by tightening their bottoms. This can make them very uncomfortable. One way to help a baby release that gas is to place him in a knee-chest position. Place his back against your chest and pull his knees up to his chest.

Diapering

Diapering can seem intimidating if you've never done it before, but you'll soon master the skill. There are two basic types of diapers, cloth and disposable, and several things to consider in deciding which type to use: cost, frequency of changes (cloth diapers require more frequent changes), convenience (disposable ones don't need to be laundered; cloth ones can be laundered at home or by a diaper service), and environmental concerns.

Guidelines for Diapering

• Use water and a cloth instead of commercial wipes on your newborn. The perfumes in the wipes can irritate a newborn's skin. As the baby gets older, his sensitivity to commercial wipes will decrease. We recommend that you use wipes containing lanolin.

• With a baby girl, spread the labia to clean the perineum front to back. Cleaning from the front to the back helps to prevent urinary tract and vaginal infections.

• Most pediatricians discourage the use of lotions and powders for newborns. This is because most powders contain perfumes and dyes that can cause skin irritations. Lotions can clog the baby's pores, causing skin problems. As the baby grows older, this is

less of a problem, although pediatricians may continue to recommend that you avoid commercial baby lotions and powders
containing talc and use cornstarch-based powders instead.

If the Baby Develops a Diaper Rash

• Evaluate his diet. Have you introduced him to any new foods or
drinks in the last few days? If so, discontinue the new food.

• Antibiotics may cause a diaper rash. This does not necessarily
mean that the baby is allergic to the antibiotic. It may have
changed the content and pH of his stool, which can cause skin
irritation. Do not stop the antibiotic unless your pediatrician
advises you to do so.

• Clean the diaper area with warm water only.

• If the rash is mild, over-the-counter creams or powders will usually clear it up.

• When possible, expose the area to air for thirty-minute periods.
This is especially important for more serious diaper rashes.

Call the Pediatrician If—

• The rash continues for three days or longer or gets worse.

• The skin is bleeding or has blistered areas.

• The area of the rash is swollen.

In these situations, over-the-counter creams and ointments will not help. Prescription medications are necessary.

Bathing

Bathtime is usually a pleasant experience for both you and your baby. Remember, until the umbilical cord stump falls off, give your baby sponge baths. If he has had a circumcision, don't give him a tub bath until it has completely healed.

Guidelines for Bathing

• Gather everything you need before starting the bath.

• Bathe the baby in the warmest part of the day. Keep the room warm as well.

• When sponge bathing, keep the baby covered with a blanket or towel except for the area being cleaned. Clean from top to bottom, clean to dirty. Dry him immediately. Newborns lose body heat very quickly when they're wet.

• We recommend that you use a baby tub that fits on a countertop or inside a regular tub.

• Bath water should be comfortably warm, not hot. For safety, set the water heater at a low to medium temperature. Anything higher can scald your baby. Never allow your children to play with the knobs that control the water flow.

- In the first four to six months, your baby will need support while sitting in the tub. Support him across his back, holding on to the arm farthest away from you. This allows you the greatest freedom to clean him with the most security and safety (fig. 9.5).

- *Never Leave the Baby Unattended!*

Figure 9.5

Establishing Sleep Patterns

After a couple of months, sleep-deprived parents look forward to getting a good night's rest, yet they are usually told not to expect to get uninterrupted sleep at night for six months to a year. It doesn't have to be that way. You can help your baby learn to sleep when you do. The best resource available to assist you and your baby in this all important life skill is *On Becoming Babywise* and *Babywise II*. There is a good reason why two million parents have utilized both books and the *Babywise* principles. They are medically sound, easily understood, and produce wonderful results for mom and baby in adjusting to this postpartum period.

Most newborns sleep most of the time, particularly in the first two weeks of life. How do you know what is normal and when to be concerned? If your baby wakes up every few hours, eats well, seems content, and is alert when he's awake, he is well within the norm. However, if it's difficult to wake him up for a feeding, if he's not interested in feeding, too tired to feed, or rarely alert, you are right to be concerned and should consult your pediatrician. If a baby suddenly becomes lethargic, it's a sign that something needs to be checked.

If you find that your baby has his days and nights mixed up, you can begin to teach him that nights are for sleeping and days are for playing and napping. You can do this by waking him every two-and-a-half to three hours during the day to feed and have some playtime. At night, feed him and then put him back in his crib.

A word of warning: Parents often try to keep their newborn up too long, thinking that if he stays awake longer, he'll sleep longer. That's not the case with a newborn. Instead, he will become too stimulated and have difficulty settling into sleep. After a feeding session of approximately thirty minutes, another fifteen minutes of awake time is usually enough stimulation. You might want to adjust these times to see what works best for your baby.

Sleep Position

Today's research strongly suggests, and the American Academy of Pediatrics recommends, that putting a baby on his or her back for sleep, (rather than on the baby's tummy) reduces the risk of SIDS? What is not conclusive is whether back-sleeping is the primary or secondary factor in the reduction of risk. Does the supine position (wholly on the back) remove the child from soft surfaces and gas-trapping objects (mattresses, pillows, crib liners), which could be the actual risk-factor, or is it actually the biomechanics of tummy-sleeping? More research is needed to answer that question. Meanwhile, we suggest you speak to your health care provider if you have any questions concerning SIDS and the positioning of your baby. Parents ask us if back-positioning will interfere with the establishment of healthy sleep? The answer is no.

Amount of Sleep

How much sleep does your baby need? At first, an average, healthy newborn will probably sleep about sixteen to seventeen hours a day, divided into three to four naps evenly spaced between feed-ings. Usually, one sleep period lasts four to five hours. Ideally, of course, this one occurs at night.

Once your baby begins to sleep through the night, you need to be alert to any sudden late-night awakenings to feed. Growth spurts can cause these, so you will want to add an extra feeding during the day rather than disrupt the pattern of uninterrupted nighttime sleep.

Well-Baby Care

"Well-baby" checkups are routine appointments with your pediatrician. The frequency may vary with individual doctors. Generally the appoint-ments are at two and four weeks; at two, four, six, nine, twelve, fifteen, and twenty-four months; and then annually.

During a "Well-baby" visit, the doctor will do a complete physi-cal examination of your baby. He will evaluate his height and weight and take his temperature. In the early months, he will measure the cir-cumference of his head and chest. He will ask you questions about your baby's sleep patterns, activity, diet, and appetite. The purpose of these examinations and questions is to detect any problems with his growth and development and to give you the opportunity to ask questions.

Immunizations are an important part of well-baby care. While breast milk provides the baby with certain antibodies, immunity for the baby is limited to those diseases that a mother has been exposed to. Vaccines help to protect against what have proven to be deadly ill-nesses in past generations. These illnesses include Polio, Diphtheria, Pertussis (Whooping Cough), Tetanus (lockjaw), Rubella (German Measles), Mumps, Measles (rubeola), Type-B haemophilus influenzae, and Hepatitis B. The side effects from vaccines are usually mild. Your doctor should be open to answering any questions you have about the need for, and timing of immunizations. There are currently many opinions regarding them, so you need to use wisdom and make your decision based on accurate information.

Sick-Baby Care

A sick baby can create great insecurity in parents, yet it is not uncommon for a baby to exhibit symptoms of illness as frequently as seven to nine times within his first year of life. We would like to encourage you to be thinking about preventive care.

Provide the baby with a clean, safe environment, and a routine that provides for regular sleeping, playing, and feeding. The following are reasons to call the pediatrician, especially in the first few months of the baby's life:

• rectal temperature over 100.4 degrees

• green vomit or excessive vomiting

• diarrhea: three or more stools beyond what is normal for the baby, or watery, foul-smelling stools that continue for more than forty-eight hours

• constipation: no stools for forty-eight hours, or stools that are hard and dry (do remember that breast-fed babies may have only one or two stools per week because breast milk is nearly 100 percent digested)

• yellowish skin and whites of the eyes, as this could be indicative of Jaundice

When you call the pediatrician, be prepared to answer some specific questions:

• When did the symptoms begin?

• How long have they lasted?

• When was the last feeding, stool, and wet diaper?

• Is there a rash?

• What was the baby's weight at the last visit to the pediatrician?

• What is the baby's temperature?

• How was the temperature taken—rectally (in the bottom) or axillary (in the armpit)?

Have a pen and paper ready to write down any instructions the pediatrician gives you. Precise instructions about medications are extremely important.

Taking an Accurate Temperature

Remember that external factors like hot weather or being over-dressed can influence the baby's temperature. Dehydration, immunizations, and teething may also cause a low-grade fever (99 to 100 degrees).

- *To take an axillary temperature:* Place the tip of the thermometer under the baby's arm, close to the armpit (axilla), and hold his arm in place so the thermometer can respond to his body heat. It may take two to three minutes to get an accurate reading. An axillary temperature is adequate for a baby under four weeks old; after that, a rectal reading is preferable. An axillary temperature is usually two degrees lower than a rectal temperature.

- *To take a rectal temperature:* Coat the tip of the thermometer with Vaseline or water-soluble lubricant before inserting it inside the baby's rectum. To keep from damaging the tissue, you should insert the thermometer no more than three-quarters of an inch into the rectum. An accurate reading should occur within one to two minutes after insertion. The normal range for a rectal temperature is 97 to 99 degrees, or one degree higher than a temperature taken orally. A rectal temperature should be taken until the child is able to safely hold the thermometer under his tongue (approximately age three).

Useful Items to Have on Hand When a Baby is Sick
- A rectal, digital, or ear thermometer.

- A cool-mist vaporizer for use when the baby is congested or has a respiratory infection. The mist helps to loosen and liquefy secretions, which is especially helpful if the baby has croup. A vaporizer can also be effective in treating a fever, as the mist can help cool the baby.

- A medicine syringe, medicine dropper, and measuring spoon are helpful in measuring small doses of liquid oral medications.

• Liquid acetaminophen (Tylenol) is recommended in infant dosages for treatment of pain and fever (when the baby's temperature is over 101 degrees). Consult your pediatrician for the proper dosage for your baby, as it will vary according to his age and height. Throughout childhood, the dosage should be according to body-size, not age. Your doctor may also say it's okay to use ibuprofen, but *do not give aspirin to children of any age.*

• Liquid decongestants are sold over the counter. Consult your pediatrician about which one to use and the correct dosage. Decongestants are not recommended for children under two years of age.

• A bulb syringe helps suck mucus out of the baby's nostrils. With a cold or respiratory infection, a baby's nose fills with mucus, and because a baby breathes through his nose, it's important to keep his nasal passages clear. The hospital will probably send a bulb syringe home with you. If not, you can purchase one at any pharmacy.

As you look ahead to the next milestone in your baby's growth, try to find ways to encourage his development through activities and toys. Appendix H, "Encouraging Your Infant's Growth and Development," lists some of the basic abilities your baby will develop in his first year and some ways you can help strengthen them.

Chapter Ten

Feeding Your Baby

Your baby's body will change constantly during the first year of his life. Within twelve months, the average baby grows about ten inches, and his weight triples. At birth, he can barely lift his head, but at a year he is walking and holding toys. Proper nutrition is essential to support this rapid growth.

The first decision you need to make about your baby's nutrition is whether to breast or bottle-feed. The decision should be a mutual one by both parents, as there are advantages and disadvantages to both methods. Also keep in mind the possibility of combining the two types of feeding to blend the advantages of each. Please remember, this chapter is not a substitute for the wonderful information found in *On Becoming Babywise*. We introduce it here with the single goal of acquainting you with some of the basic activities associated with nurturing your newborn.

Breast-Feeding Advantages

The advantages of breast-feeding are that breast-milk is an easily digested, economical source of all the nutrients essential for infant growth. The milk goes directly to the baby and contains natural factors that help your baby resist infection. Food allergies are not as common among infants who are breast-fed. Breast-feeding is also good for you. It helps you lose weight and return your uterus to its normal size. It's convenient, as there is there is no preparation or heating time.

However, it is not always convenient to breast-feed in public, as it may be difficult to find privacy when it is time to nurse. You also may not feel as free to leave your baby with a sitter at feeding times, and because your prolactin levels are high while you're nursing, you may find that you have less sexual desire.

The advantage of bottle-feeding is that anyone can feed the baby at any time, which allows you to leave the baby with a sitter when necessary. Still, formula can be costly, and it takes time to prepare. Prepared formula that is not used immediately must be refrigerated, and storage time is limited to between twenty-four and forty-eight hours.

Because of additives, formulas contain most of the nutrients the baby needs, but the preparation process can destroy some of the vitamins and minerals. Digestive problems are common with the use of formula, and food allergies may be more apparent. You may find that you need to try several brands before you find the right match for your baby's digestive system.

As you evaluate how each feeding method will best fit into your family's routine, ask yourself these questions:

• Does our family schedule allow for adequate rest and proper nutrition for a breast-feeding mom?

• Will we routinely leave the baby with a sitter?

• Is our family routinely in public situations where breast-feeding may not be practical?

• Does Dad have a strong preference?

Bottle-Feeding and Formula

There are many types of formula on the market. Your pediatrician is the best source of information about which is best suited to your baby's needs.

Most formulas come in a variety of forms; powdered, concentrate, or ready-to-serve. Read the package and follow the directions for preparation. Improper mixing can cause digestive problems. If you are using a formula that requires you to add water—use bottled; sterile water; or boil tap water for five minutes, allow it to cool, and then use it as directed.

Bottles and nipples must be cleaned properly. Automatic dishwashers do a good job of cleaning and sterilizing. If a dishwasher is not available—wash the bottles and nipples in hot, soapy water (use a bottle and nipple brush to clean the crevices), rinse with boiling water, and allow them to dry.

Feeding Tips

Formula should be given warm, as cold formula can cause cramping and gas. Test a drop of the formula on the inside of your wrist to make sure it is not too warm. Do not microwave formula, as it can create hot areas in the formula that can burn the baby. Burp the baby halfway through and at the completion of each feeding. Failure to burp him adequately can also cause cramping and gas. Newborns usually feed every two-and-a-half to three hours. The following table gives an estimate of the amount of formula the baby will need per feeding as he grows.

Age of Infant	Ounces/Feeding	Feedings/Day
Newborn to 2 weeks	1.5 to 3 ounces	8 to 10
2 weeks to 2 months	3 to 5 ounces	7 to 8
2 months	5 ounces	7 to 8
3 months	6 to 6.5 ounces	6 to 7
4 months to 6 months	7 to 8 ounces	4 to 6

When to Call the Doctor

Consult your pediatrician if the baby has any of these feeding problems:

- vomiting
- diarrhea
- colic
- unusual rash
- constipation

Breast-Feeding

During your pregnancy, hormonal changes in your body prepared your breasts for lactation. You probably noticed most of the following changes:

- The veins became more visible.

• The breasts and nipples became larger.

• Stretch marks appeared.

• The areola became larger and darker in color.

• Sweat glands in the areola became more prominent and active.

Figure 10.1

• Colostrum leaked prior to the delivery of your baby.

During pregnancy, the pituitary gland releases the hormone prolactin, but estrogen levels block its action. After the delivery of the baby, estrogen levels decrease, allowing the prolactin levels to increase, and lactation occurs.

Since the estrogen level needs to drop and the prolactin level needs to rise following delivery of the baby, milk is not produced immediately. For the first three to four days after delivery, the breasts produce only colostrum. When they begin to secrete milk, your breasts may be full and tender. Your body may ache, and your temperature might rise. The baby's sucking stimulates the nerve endings and promotes more prolactin secretion and, therefore, more milk. It also causes the release of oxytocin, which causes the ejection of the milk, or the "let-down reflex."

Keys to Success

The following conditions are necessary for successful breast-feeding:

• a mother who is mentally and physically healthy

- a proper latching-on and let-down reflex
- a baby who can suck adequately
- an adequate blood supply to the breasts
- milk ducts free of obstruction
- regular feedings
- complete emptying of both breasts with each feeding

Your overall good health is very important. Your diet has to meet your own nutritional needs as well as provide adequate nutrition for your baby. That's why you should continue to take prenatal vitamins while you're nursing. You should also increase your fluid intake to accommodate the production of milk. Drinking an added glass of water with each feeding will help you do this.

Feeding Techniques

Breast-feeding requires patience. It may take a couple of weeks before you become comfortable with the techniques. At first, organize your daily schedule to eliminate outside activities, and then gradually return to them. Minimize stress whenever possible, and breast-feed the baby in a quiet area where there are limited opportunities for interruptions.

The average nursing period for a newborn will usually be around thirty minutes. Some babies may nurse in less than thirty minutes and some may nurse longer. Try to get a full feeding in each nursing cycle, allowing the baby to empty one breast before moving to the other. A healthy, full-term newborn can accomplish this in fifteen minutes. Once you and your baby have settled into a comfortable nursing routine, spending much longer than thirty minutes at a feeding will encourage him to suck less vigorously and to use your breast as a pacifier. With proper technique, a baby can empty a breast in five to ten minutes.

Hearing and seeing the baby swallow (along with the tingling sensation you feel when milk is released) are good indications that your baby is receiving adequate nutrition.

Start with alternate sides at each feeding. For example, start on the left side and finish on the right side. For the next feeding, start on the right side and finish on the left. (Hint: Pin a safety pin to the bra strap of the side the baby nursed last.) This helps to ensure complete emptying of the breasts and equal milk production in both.

Figure 10.2

Put your baby in a "heart-to-heart" position, with his tummy toward yours (fig. 10.2). Hold your breast with your thumb on top and your fingers underneath in a "C" position, being careful not to place your fingers over the areola.

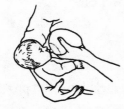

Figure 10.3

Gently tickle the baby's lower lip with the nipple until he opens his mouth wide (fig.10.3). Pull him to your breast, keeping him in the tummy-to-tummy position. This allows the baby to latch on to the entire nipple and most of the areola (figs. 10.4 and 10.5).

Figure 10.4

Figure 10.5

To remove your baby from the breast, gently insert your finger into the corner of his mouth to release the suction and move him away from you (fig.10.6). Be sure to burp him after he feeds at each breast. Use different positions

Figure 10.6

Figure 10.8

for breast-feeding, including the side-lying position (fig.10.7) and the football hold (fig.10.8).

Breast-Feeding Tips

Wear comfortable clothing that allows for easy access and modesty during feeding. A well-fitting nursing bra is

Figure 10.7

a must. At the end of the feeding, pat the milk off both areolae (the area surrounding the nipples) and allow your breasts to dry completely. This helps soothe and heal sore nipples. If air-drying takes too long, you can use a blow-dryer set on warm.

Leaking of breast-milk is common during the first few weeks. Use breast pads (without plastic lining) to protect your clothing, and protect the bed mattress with a waterproof pad. Once you establish a feeding routine, leaking will decrease. Wearing a soft bra to bed also helps prevent nighttime leaking.

Expressing Milk

Occasionally it may be necessary to express, or withdraw, milk from the breast. Reasons for this vary from medical necessity to convenience. Some examples of medical necessity are cases of engorgement, blocked milk-ducts, breast infection, cracked nipples, or too much milk. It may also be necessary to stimulate milk production or to maintain adequate milk supply for a sick baby. An example of expressing for convenience is storing breast milk if you and your baby will be separated at the designated feeding time. After nursing is well-established, occasionally offer the baby a bottle of pumped breast-milk (or formula) to encourage the baby to learn to take a bottle as well.

Before expressing milk, be sure to wash your hands thoroughly and rinse your breasts with water. Cleanliness is very important. All items that come in contact with the breast-milk should be sterilized. This includes bottles, jars, covers, and the parts of the breast pump. If a dishwasher is not available, boil the items for twenty minutes to sterilize them, and then allow them to air dry.

For manual expression, place your fingers under the breast for support, with your thumb on top, and then compress by sliding your thumb toward the nipple (approximately thirty times per minute).

Although you can express your milk manually, mechanical expression is easier and more effective. Have a breast pump on hand before the baby is born. To use a hand pump, support the breast by placing your hand under it and use your fingers to hold the flanged end of the pump over the areola. Use your other hand to gently and rhythmically pump the slide or plunger. If you use an electric pump, follow the instructions for the type of appliance you are using.[10]

Once the milk is expressed, pour it into a sterile container and cover it. Plastic bags such as Playtex sterile bags are preferable to glass bottles. If you plan to feed the expressed milk to the baby within twenty-four hours, store it in the refrigerator. If the milk will be given to the baby later than that, store it in the freezer.

Breast-milk can be stored in the freezer for up to six months at a temperature of eighteen degrees or colder. To prevent waste, freeze two to three ounces per bag. When you are ready to use a bag, defrost it in the refrigerator or thaw it quickly by standing the sealed bag in a pan of warm water. Gradually increase the temperature of the water until the milk has liquefied and warmed to body temperature. Separation of breast milk in layers is normal, so knead the bag to thoroughly mix the milk. Do not microwave breast milk, as that can destroy some of its infection-fighting properties.

Use the entire amount of defrosted milk within twenty-four hours. The unused portion cannot be refrozen. Once the milk has touched the baby's mouth in the bottle, assume that the milk is contaminated, and don't give him any of the unused portion. (This is also true for formula.)

Do not store or give the baby any milk collected from a plastic breast shield. There is an increased possibility of contamination of milk expressed this way, and it has fewer calories.

The best time to pump is following a feeding, particularly after the first morning feeding when your milk supply is the greatest.

Breast-Feeding Problems and Solutions

As They Relate to the Baby

A sleepy baby has a tendency not to nurse adequately, and he may not take enough milk during each feeding to allow for adequate intervals between feedings. Changing, unwrapping, or undressing him can help wake him up. As a last resort, you can place a cool, damp washcloth on his feet.

If your baby is underweight or losing weight, have your pediatrician evaluate him for medical problems. If the examination doesn't reveal an underlying medical condition, consider giving him supplemental feedings. (For example, breast-feed in the morning, bottle-feed mid-morning, nurse in the afternoon, bottle-feed at dinnertime, and nurse at bedtime.) You also might want to consult someone who specializes in lactation counseling. Most hospitals can refer you to a lactation consultant. Using a device called Lact-Aids might help you maintain an adequate milk supply.[11]

If your baby was born prematurely or is ill and you are not sure if he will be able to nurse adequately, consult your pediatrician. Even if he can not nurse initially, he may be able to as he grows or as the medical condition is resolved. If this is the case, you can express your breast-milk and store it for later use.

As They Relate to the Mother

Breast-feeding problems are not solely caused by an infant. There are some related problems including:

Engorged Breasts

Engorgement usually occurs when the milk supply comes in on the third or fourth day after delivery. It can also occur during the first four to six weeks after delivery if the baby is bottle-fed for a feeding or if you don't empty both breasts at each feeding. It may be necessary to nurse the baby more frequently (every two and a half hours) until the engorgement passes. Be sure to offer both breasts, and to alternate sides. To completely empty the breasts, express the milk manually or with a pump or take a warm shower to allow the remaining milk to flow.

Tender, Lumpy, or Painful Breasts

Your breasts may feel this way as your body learns to produce milk based on a regular routine, or even after your milk supply is established. A tight-fitting bra might be the problem, so use one that fits properly or a nursing bra. Most maternity stores will advise you on a proper fit. Offer both breasts at each feeding, alternate sides at the beginning of each feeding, and allow five to ten minutes of nursing on each side to ensure the breasts are completely emptied.

Mastitis

This is an infection that can lead to fever and other flu-like symptoms. Your temperature may rise at each feeding. The infection may be due to cracked nipples, which allow bacteria to enter through the hard, reddened cracks in the skin, or it may be due to a plugged milk-duct caused by a bra that is too tight. (A rule of thumb is that if the bra creeps up when you lift your arms, you are at risk for a blocked duct.) An underwire bra might also be a problem. Occasionally, a laboratory culture is taken of the baby's mouth to determine if an organism is causing the infection.

Maintain your nursing routine, wear a well-fitted bra, eat a well-balanced diet, drink lots of fluids, and get plenty of rest. For aches or fever, take Tylenol. Your doctor may also prescribe antibiotics.

Plugged Duct

A tender, sore area or a lump on the breast indicates that a duct may be plugged due to irregular or incomplete emptying of the milk. Milk is unable to pass through the duct and accumulates, causing swelling. Keep nipples and areolae clean. Using warm water, wash any dried material off the nipples. Apply heat to the area before nursing, and begin nursing first on the affected side. Maintain your nursing routine and get adequate rest.

Inverted Nipples

Inverted nipples are flat or retracted into the breast. The difficulty may accompany the soreness caused by engorgement, or it may be a condition that is noticed prior to delivery. It makes breast-feeding difficult because the baby has a harder time latching on, a problem that is intensified by poor technique. Initially, pump the breasts briefly before the baby latches on. It takes patience and persistence to correct latching-on difficulties.

If the condition is apparent before delivery, gently rolling the nipple between your thumb and forefinger may help pull out your nipples. After delivery, ask your doctor or the nurses at the hospital for help. Use breast shields if your caregiver advises you to, and avoid using supplemental bottles until breast-feeding is well-established.

Sore Nipples

Tender nipples may be caused by poor positioning technique, so you should review the section on proper technique on page 151. You will notice the soreness mostly when your baby first latches on, but the discomfort could continue during the entire feeding. The soreness may be due to breast engorgement; the baby latching-on to only the nipple instead of to both the nipple and the areola; improperly removing him from the breast; or allowing him to nurse too long. The tenderness may last from four to six weeks.

Rotate starting sides to distribute the sucking, nursing last on the side that is sorest. Slowly build up to ten minutes on each side. Do not use nursing pads with plastic linings. Alternate positions so that the pressure doesn't always fall on the same part of the nipple. After nursing, clean your nipples (with warm water only), or leave the milk on and allow them to air dry. Use small amounts of Vitamin E oil, lanolin, or breast cream and pain medication as prescribed by your doctor.

Cracked Nipples (Also see Sore Nipples.)

If your nipples have deep cracks, bleed, and are tender and sore, do not nurse the baby for one to two days. Express the breast-milk instead.

Too Much Milk

In this condition, your breasts refill quickly after feeding, and the milk flows from the nipples between feedings. This can be caused by the production of large amounts of milk before your body adjusts the amount to your baby's needs, and it can result in over-feeding or feeding too frequently. Reduce the amount of time the baby nurses at each breast. To slow the flow of milk, do not pump the excess after feedings.

Not Enough Milk

Poor milk production may be due to poor breast development, poor general health, poor diet, inadequate fluid intake, or lack of rest. It can also occur if you are over-anxious, tense, or apprehensive; or if you give supplemental bottles several times a day. Your baby may cry between feedings and have symptoms such as vomiting and abnormal stools, vigorous sucking on the hand or pacifier, weight loss, lack of adequate urine output, dehydration, or constipation.

Nurse your baby every two-and-a-half to three hours for approximately fifteen minutes on each side. Feed in a quiet area and relax during feedings. Seek treatment for physical discomforts that do not allow you to relax. Express milk after each feeding. Maintain adequate nutritional and fluid intake. Get eight hours of sleep at night and take a nap during the day.

Weaning

Weaning is a gradual process of decreasing the number of feedings per day until nursing stops. It usually begins when solid foods are introduced, which can be as early as four months. As the amount of solid foods eaten increases, the amount of milk your baby needs decreases.

Your baby's pediatrician should recommend when to begin solid foods, as well as the kind and amount. The usual recommended order is cereal, vegetables, meats, and then fruits. Many pediatricians think that because fruits are sweet, they should be offered last.

We recommend that when you introduce a new food, you do not add another new one for a minimum of three to five days. This helps you identify food sensitivities, which may manifest themselves as mouth-sores, a rash around the mouth, diaper rash, hives, diarrhea, vomiting, or excessive gas. If a sensitivity does occur, do not give the food again until the pediatrician allows it. If the baby develops hives, notify your pediatrician immediately.

Give your baby yellow vegetables such as carrots, squash, and sweet potatoes no more than two to four times a week. Yellow vegetables contain carotene, which can build up in the baby's body and cause the skin to have an orange-yellow hue. Be aware that baby foods labeled "mixed vegetables" contain a large quantity of yellow vegetables. Once the baby is well-established on solid foods and has an adequate number of teeth, you can begin introducing table foods. Food grinders and blenders give foods a soft consistency that allows the baby to eat them without difficulty.

Discontinuation of breast-feeding shouldn't be abrupt. The milk supply has taken time to be built up, and it will take time to diminish. The easiest feedings to drop are those that occur later in the day.

Decide which feeding to drop and be consistent. Offer juice or formula in place of the missed feeding. Your breasts will be fuller and may be uncomfortable when it's time for the next feeding, but after two or three days, your body will adjust, and the discomfort will not be as noticeable. Continue to drop feedings as your milk supply and the baby adjust until he is completely weaned.

Chapter Eleven

Birth Through Adoption

Some children become part of a family not through pregnancy and childbirth, but through the legal process of adoption—in which birth-parents relinquish their child to others who raise him as their own. Adoptions are often the result of difficult circumstances, and as such, they are a mixture of gain and loss. As we consider the adoption process, we'll look at some of the circumstances that often surround the lives of people who decide to adopt and parents who decide to give their child up for adoption. If you find yourself in one of these groups, the information we provide can help you make wise decisions.

The Decision to Adopt

In most cases, the decision to pursue adoption follows a diagnosis of infertility. If you have unsuccessfully pursued infertility treatment, adopting a child may be a high priority for you. But before moving toward adoption, you need to put the infertility issue to rest by asking yourself why you want to add a child to your family. It must be at least as important to you to have an adopted child *as your own* as it was to have a biological child *of your own.*

A single person contemplating adoption must also consider his or her motives. In modern American society, it can be easy to view parenting as just another pursuit at which to succeed. Sometimes an individual's personal agenda has nothing to do with what would be in the best interest of an adopted child. If you are a single person thinking about adopting, ask yourself the following questions:

- Is my desire to adopt a child driven by a wish to help a child who would otherwise be homeless?
- Would I be willing to accept a child of any age, or am I really only interested in a baby or a young child?
- Will I be able to provide a secure foundation for a child without the help of a spouse?
- Would marriage compromise my commitment to the child?

People thinking about adopting also need to consider the financial burden it will impose, as the cost will go into the thousands of dollars before the adoption is final.

At some point after you examine your reasons for wanting to adopt and your resources for carrying it through, you will make the decision either to proceed or not. Realize that just as there is often no "good" time to get pregnant, there may be no "good" time to pursue adoption. Life doesn't just come to a halt after you decide to adopt. All the other circumstances of your life—your finances, career, family interactions, and the like, are occurring simultaneously.

Once you have made the connections needed to follow through with an adoption, you will face unique challenges. One difficulty is not having the time to prepare that a nine-month pregnancy provides. As an adoptive parent, you may not have the luxury of making physical preparations for the child because you must be willing to act on the opportunity should a child become available.

You also may have to make a sudden decision about your job and if, and when you should discuss the possible adoption with your employer. Caring for a new child is physically and emotionally demanding for anyone; yet family, friends, and coworkers may not fully understand your needs.

Ways to Adopt

When you long for a child, you may feel like knocking on every door possible to find one! There are several ways you can link up with birth-parents.

Foster Parenting

The purpose of a foster home is to provide a stable home environment for a child from a troubled home. Usually there is an ongoing relationship with the biological parents, such as weekend visits. The goal in many cases is to put the child back in the home of origin when the circumstances are safe and healthy. Foster parenting may lead to adoption, but no one should become a foster parent with that end in view.

Independent Adoption

Independent, or private, adoption is a means for adoptive parents to actively participate in the search for a child. Serving as a mediator, a lawyer puts the individuals in contact with each other. Résumés describing the couple and their goals may be sent out to hospitals, health-care providers, and friends who might become resources for adoption.

Most private adoptions are open, which means the adoptive parents are in contact with the biological parents, or at least with the birth-mother. In an open adoption, the birth-mother and adoptive parents communicate in some way before the birth of the baby and share in the transition of the baby's becoming part of the new family. That might mean having telephone conversations, seeing pictures or a videotape of the adoptive couple's home environment, or meeting them in person.

One of the advantages of open adoption is that it allows the parties to try to match the physical characteristics of those involved so that the child will look something like the adoptive parents. Another benefit is that more babies are available through open adoption, so it's possible to link up an appropriate couple and a birth-mother relatively quickly. All the paperwork can be done within nine months.

On the downside, negotiating the details of an open adoption can be a delicate matter. Everyone is apt to feel tremendously vulnerable during the transition. If you are adopting, your wishes may not coincide with those of the birth-mother. You might hope that she would let you be there for the birth, but she might not want that. You might not want her to receive any medication in labor that could affect "your baby," but that's a decision for the birth-mother to make.

The estimated cost for an open adoption agreement varies from state to state. It may be as low as $3,000 or as high as $25,000, depending on the couple's preferences and the attorney's fees. You would also be responsible for covering the birth-mother's costs incurred during the pregnancy and up to the time the adoption is final. That could be an additional $1,800 to $5,000, depending on where you live, and it could include covering her living expenses for a few months, depending on her needs.

The major risk of an open adoption is that the birth-mother might decide to reclaim the child prior to the closure of the legal agreement. Approximately 15 percent of birth-mothers change their mind about the adoption. Fortunately, most of the time this occurs at the time of delivery, not afterwards. Laws vary from state to state regarding the finalization of adoption. It can take anywhere from ten days to a year before a child is legally considered adopted. This is a time of tremendous vulnerability, and it can be unnerving for everyone. If the birth-mother changes her mind, you cannot recover the money you have paid out to that point (adoption insurance is available but expensive). And, having invested much more than money, this outcome can be a devastating blow to your hopes.

Adoption Agencies

In addition to state agencies, there are various state-licensed religious and secular agencies that place children in adoptive homes.[12] Such adoptions are almost always "closed," which means a legal representative of the agency makes all the arrangements.

You have to be persistent and patient when dealing with public and private agencies. All agencies will thoroughly investigate you—including your history of previous marriages and your finances, and will evaluate your home life before placing you on a waiting list. Once you're on the list, the wait for an infant could go on for years, although you might be able to adopt an older child or one with special needs sooner. In the latter case, you would need to carefully consider the greater financial commitment it would take to provide for a child with medical or emotional challenges. Agencies tend to depend on the age and financial status of a couple to determine if they will be able to provide a secure home for the child. Often there is an age-limit of forty, which can make adoption difficult for a capable older couple.

The agency will often match the birth-mother's desires with those of the adoptive family. In fact, many birth-mothers are involved in choosing the adoptive family. After the birth of the baby, the mother relinquishes her legal parental rights to the agency, which gives the adoptive parents the security of knowing that the birth-mother cannot change her mind about the adoption later.

International Adoption

As the world has become smaller and the doors of communication have opened wider in impoverished countries, international adoptions have become increasingly common. The biggest deterrent to pursuing international adoption is the tremendous amount of red tape involved in bringing a foreign child into the United States. In some cases, you will need to travel to the country to obtain the child, and you may find agreements vague and sometimes unreliable when you deal with other cultures.

The wait for international adoption could be one to two years. The paperwork usually includes a home study (which usually takes three months), FBI and police clearance (including fingerprints), and clearance through the Immigration and Naturalization Service (INS). Everything must be authenticated and notarized at the embassy of the country of the child's origin and translated into the language of that country. An international adoption often costs as much as a domestic adoption. Paperwork and travel expenses can cost between $15,000 and $25,000.

All children entering the United States must have medical clearance, so health problems may prevent an adoption from going through. In general, the more rural the area the child is from, the less chance there is for high-risk problems. Life in a crowded city tends to be characterized by increased drug use and sexually-transmitted infections that can affect the children. Many of the children have lived in institutions. The time and emotions invested in pursuing an international adoption could mean heartache if medical issues prevent the child from entering the United States.

On the other hand, the sheer number of children from other countries needing placement holds out great hope to an adoptive couple, especially one that has had trouble adopting in America. An international adoption can be a positive experience for a family that embraces the adopted child's culture. And there will be fewer emotional issues arising from involvement with the birth-mother because of the separation imposed by distance.

After the Adoption Is Final

If infertility was once your primary focus, there may be a tendency for you to make the child the focus of the family. If you do, you'll reap the common consequences of child-centered parenting, and the child may use the issue of adoption as a way to manipulate you. The same thing is true for both biological and adoptive families: The child is to be a welcome member of the family, but not the center of it.

There are so many unknowns along the way. You may never have reliable information about the medical history or inherited traits of your adopted child, particularly if it was a closed adoption. As people offer you opinions based on their own experiences, you could become confused and anxious. You may fear that you will lose the child through illness or because the birth-mother changes her mind. Or you may fear that the child will reject you when he gets older.

The desire to experience things a biological parent would experience is normal, and some women who adopt infants wish to breast-feed. Although it's difficult, this can be accomplished through devices that allow the baby to receive formula while nursing at the breast. However, being a good mother is not tied to the ability to breast-feed. Bonding occurs over time and does not depend solely on what occurs during the few moments after birth or on whether or not a mother breast-feeds. The attachment to the child will deepen with time, just as it does with a biological child. Most adoptive parents choose to bottle-feed their infants.

There are other considerations for the adoptive family, such as adding to a family with natural children. The idea of integrating a new child into the family requires honesty from each family member. The decision of when and how to tell a child that he is adopted is very personal. A child from another country may look very different from the other family members, and that might make it necessary to talk about the adoption early on. It can be extremely traumatic for a child to suddenly find out from someone else that he is adopted. The basic trust in his parents may be destroyed, and restored only with difficulty.

As the child grows, he may be curious about the circumstances of his adoption. He may wonder why his birth-parents did not choose to raise him. He may want to know about his parents' ethnic backgrounds and what they looked like. It will be helpful for you to have as much information as possible about the birth-parents, and it's generally best to be honest when questions arise and not to keep the adoption a secret. Wisdom would dictate that as a couple you discuss beforehand how to answer your child's questions and prepare yourself for how you will react if your child desires to contact his birth-parents.

When talking to your child about his birth, emphasize that his birth-mother wanted him, but that she knew she was not able to provide him with the best home environment. Because of her love for him, she put his best interest first and provided the gift of a child through adoption to another family that strongly desired to have a child of their own.

Adoptive parents need to demonstrate sensitivity not only about how much and what information to share, but when. The timing needs to reflect the child's stage of emotional growth. Revealing the details of a child's adoption requires discernment and sensitivity on the part of the parents and other family members.

The Decision to Release a Child for Adoption

A child who is placed for adoption was most likely born in the midst of difficult circumstances. Although the physical union that brought about the conception of the child may have been based on a loving relationship, the parents might not have had the resources they needed to raise a child. A couple faced with an unplanned pregnancy may find little support for their decision to place the baby for adoption, depending on the reaction of family and friends, and whether the couple is married or not. Pregnancy Resource Centers try to fill the gap by providing services such as pregnancy testing, prenatal care, referrals, housing, daily living support, and personal counseling. Many churches also see this as an area of ministry.

The birth-father's reaction and involvement differs from person to person. The stereotypical view is that an unwed birth-father is not concerned about his child's fate. Some, however, are very concerned and want to be involved in the pregnancy and the decisions regarding the child. A father should not be denied the opportunity to deal with the issues surrounding his child's life.

In evaluating what is best for the baby, both birth-parents should ask themselves these questions:

• What are my responsibilities in this situation?
• What impact will my decisions have on this child?
• What impact will these decisions have on my education, career, and family?

At times, a birth-father may decide to assume responsibility for the baby. His role in the child's life needs to be clearly established. He will either need to legally agree to support the child financially, or relinquish his rights in the case of adoption. If the birth-father is not known or is not named, a legal petition to terminate his rights can be filed.

If the decision is to release the child for adoption, a flood of emotional issues may come into play for the birth-mother such as:

• Who will raise my baby?
• Will I ever see him again?
• Will he know who I am and why I chose to place him for adoption?
• What will become of me after this chapter in my life?
• Will I regret this decision?

If you decide to give your baby up for adoption, you may feel that you are a cold, uncaring, selfish person. Realize, however, that allowing your baby to be adopted is in essence a loving act. Try to surround yourself with people who understand that and respect your decision.

Young, Pregnant, and Alone

For an unwed pregnant teenager, the decision to give up her baby for adoption may be complicated by the reasons she chose to become sexually-active outside of marriage. Was she searching for acceptance or meaning in her life? Was she trying to fill that void with the love of a boyfriend? Did she believe that having a baby would give her something to love?

In some cases, an unwed mother will carry denial about the pregnancy and the need to change her life plans at the same time she is carrying the baby. She receives no prenatal care and perhaps even goes through labor and delivery in secrecy, only to shock family and friends with the news that a baby has just been born. If you find yourself in this situation, you may need extensive counseling to unravel such problematic thinking.

The problems associated with sexually-active teens and teenage pregnancy are numerous and deep-seated. Statistics show that only 50 percent of teenage mothers and 70 percent of teenage fathers will finish high school and that 90 percent of mothers under the age of sixteen will never finish high school. Even if the teenage parents decide to marry and keep their child, these statistics do not bode well for the future of the child.

When a pregnant teenager decides to have the baby and raise it by herself, the outlook is even dimmer. Statistics indicate that 67 percent of single-parent teenagers live below the officially designated poverty level. Statistics also show that when children of single teenage parents grow up, they are more likely to become teenage parents themselves, receive welfare, and become divorced. Instead of learning from their parents' poor choices, they are more apt to repeat them.

If you are unmarried and pregnant, you need to understand these potential pitfalls and what will be expected of you should you decide to raise your child alone. You will need wise counsel, but you should not be forced to make a decision you will later regret. You need to be sure that the decision you make is best for everyone involved. It may be helpful for you to talk with people who have placed children for adoption, adoptive parents, and adopted children to gain insight before you decide. Your decision needs to be based on fact, not feelings, so you will not waiver once your decision has been made.

As you ponder your choice, you'll need to seek prenatal care to promote a healthy outcome for both yourself and the baby. The ambivalence you may feel when you perceive fetal movement is an example of the emotional process pregnancy may be for you. Any complications during the pregnancy could further cloud your decision regarding adoption. You may begin to feel vulnerable as the life within you grows and you realize that you are more than a vessel in which this life is developing. You are the mother, and your body is responding to the changes your baby's growth is causing within you. Stretch marks, an altered body image, and scars will become permanent physical reminders of your pregnancy.

Along with the emotional issues that accompany an unplanned pregnancy come practical concerns. If you decide to release your child for adoption, you'll need to decide if you want it to be open or closed, and as the time for the birth approaches, you'll have to make plans based on the arrangements for the adoption. Here are some questions you'll want to ask yourself:

- How much do I want the birth-father to be involved?
- Do I want the adoptive parents with me during labor and birth?
- Do I want to see the baby, hold him, name him, or nurse him?
- Do I want to go to another floor after the birth?
- Do I want visitors or phone calls?

Preparing for the labor and birth may heighten the awkwardness of your circumstances. The presence of the baby's father or a supportive friend to act as a coach can make childbirth classes easier to bear, and in some cases, private childbirth classes may be preferable. Each childbirth class takes on its own personality, and your situation can create an atmosphere of honesty and sympathy in which the class members rally around you. Discussing your feelings and needs outside of class can also be a tremendous avenue of support. Faithful friends and family who are willing to rally around you can bring some stability into your life at a very bewildering time.

Your perception of pain may be different from a woman who will have the reward of having her baby at the end of labor. A Cesarean Section might seem like an easy alternative if you want to avoid a long labor and all the memories associated with it, but the risk of present and future complications from such major surgery is reason enough not to make that an automatic choice.

For some birth-mothers, contact with the baby makes the coming separation more difficult. In any case, relinquishing your baby to the adoptive couple will be very difficult emotionally. Last-minute regrets, hopes, fears, and grief will be another hurdle to get over. Supportive family or friends nearby will help make this time a little easier for you.

Leaving the hospital after your baby has been given over to the adoptive parents may make you feel as if a death has occurred, and regret may linger until the legal agreement is final. Grief is to be expected, but knowing that you have made a wise decision that is best for you and your baby, will allow the healing process to begin.

Chapter Twelve

A Word to Dads

So far in *On Becoming Birthwise*, we have been speaking mostly to moms, as they are the ones whose bodies undergo pregnancy and childbirth. But now we'd like to take a minute to speak with dads. Now that you have a new family member, we would like to remind you of an important principle that you will need to keep in mind in the years ahead: The husband-wife bond is the primary relationship in the family. Parents exercise the greatest influence on their children not in their role as a father or mother, but as a husband or wife. Today, many parents see the marriage union as the priority relationship only *before* they have children, and the result is that we live in a society characterized by child-centeredness. That's a dangerous start to parenting.

Excellence in parenting is based on the fact that children are to be welcome members of the family, not the center of it. When you strengthen your marriage, you strengthen your family. Harmony in your relationship with your wife infuses stability into the family and provides a haven of security for your children. The best way to show love to your children is to love your spouse.

Straight From a Dad's Heart

This is what went through one husband's mind while he was preparing for the transition to fatherhood:

"I have been married for a while now. I have just recently begun to feel comfortable with my role as husband. Now, all of a sudden, I am feeling the weight of responsibility on my shoulders! I think to myself, *I am responsible for this woman's happiness and well-being. I'm too young for this! I don't know what I'm doing. How did my Dad manage to do this?* But, you know, he did manage somehow.

Surprisingly, I have managed to learn a few skills when it comes to being a good husband, provider, and friend. My life is settling down. I've become more sure of myself and my role in all this. And then, the exciting news is revealed! I am going to be a dad! Dad? *I don't know how to be a dad*, I think to myself. *I feel awkward around babies. How do you hold them, anyway?*

But Dad managed, obviously, or I wouldn't be here. Dad is "Dad." He is a natural at these things, right? Well, at least I've got some time to get ready!

What has happened since getting married? More responsibility, a maturity in relating to my wife, a new understanding for my own father. Now it is time to develop the skills of being a husband, father, and leader of my growing family. All at the same time!"

If you are a man expecting your first child, there are some things you need to consider. The first, of course, is that the husband-wife relationship is the primary family relationship and that the parent-child relationship will depend on it. The months before the birth of your first child will be some of the last times you and your wife will be alone together for many years to come. Take time to build memories.

During your wife's pregnancy, you need to be keenly aware of her changing physical and emotional needs. Physically, she will become more restricted in her mobility and less comfortable, especially near the latter part of the pregnancy. She will be sensitive about her changing body shape and more apt to be hurt by teasing. Though most of the changes will be temporary, some won't.

Toward the end of the pregnancy, your role as a coach will become more and more important. You'll be training with your wife for childbirth. You should watch to be sure she doesn't injure herself around the house or at work. During the days right before the birth, you should see that she conserves energy instead of trying to clean the entire house because she knows you won't do it while she's in the hospital. Promise her you will—and then keep your promise! Perhaps you could take her out to eat, express your love for her, and share your excitement about becoming a dad.

During the actual birth process, your presence is what will reassure your wife the most. Holding her hand, stroking her hair, and massaging her back will help her to cope with the pain. You can put a cool washcloth on her forehead, give her ice chips, and read the monitor to tell her when a contraction has peaked so she can see that relief is in sight. There will come a time when your wife will not want you to leave for any reason, so you should be prepared.

While your wife is in labor, you need to be careful not to express disappointment with her lack of progress or her need for medication, anesthesia, or a Cesarean delivery. Your role at this time is as a coach, and you should be a good encourager. The goal is to have a healthy baby.

Most women never forget their childbirth experiences, and it would be a thoughtful gesture for you to give your wife a memento of the occasion—something she can keep through the years. Whenever she sees it, it will remind her of how helpful and loving her husband was.

After the baby is born, don't be surprised if no one notices you at first. Everyone will be interested in how the mother and baby are doing. The same thing will happen once you bring them home. Everyone comes to see Mom and Baby. You could dress in a clown suit and no one would notice! You might get the postpartum blues, too, but recognize that this is your lot in life for just a short time.

Once you assume your new role as "Dad," you'll need to get the baby for your wife to feed at first so she can rest as much as possible. If you don't yet know how, you should learn how to change diapers. Taking care of your child is how you will get to know your baby and begin a relationship that will last a lifetime. If Mom seems to be doing everything for the baby, perhaps you need to step in and give her a much-needed break. The goal is to be sensitive to her needs and willing to serve. After a month or so, the new mother will begin to get cabin fever, so you should get a babysitter and take her out for some time alone together.

As your child grows older, your role as trainer and coach will come into play. The saying "monkey see, monkey do" will take on a whole new meaning. You certainly won't want to be known as the Great Ape when your neighbors and friends see your kid in action! Your child is the closest reflection of you that there can be. Therefore, you'll want to model the behavior and language you want to see in him.

The old axiom "a man is the king of his castle" tells only part of the story. If the king doesn't build, repair, and protect his castle, it will come to ruin. If he doesn't remove himself from the throne to inspect the walls, take care of the queen, and make sure the moat has water in it, the hordes will take it from him.

Changing Family Relationships

Pregnancy and childbirth can bring you indescribable joy and fulfillment, but they also bring change—and change can often be perceived as loss. To avoid unrealistic expectations and potential conflict in your marriage relationship, you need to anticipate this bittersweet component of adding to your family. Remember that these challenges can lead to either positive or negative change, depending on how you react to them. Recognize and talk about your trials, and look for ways to cope with them. Learn as much as you can about them, and work together with your wife as a team to cope with them.

Since the greatest influence parents have on their children is their relationship as husband and wife, you need to make sure that your children observe you nurturing your relationship with your wife. Children can sense when their parents are not making their marriage a priority.

You need to romance your wife and occasionally take her away from things that distract her. A soothing drive to the beach, an intimate evening out at a favorite restaurant, a surprise picnic-for-two at the park, and an evening spent walking through a mall without the baby are caring ways to acknowledge your need to be alone together. Even though a baby requires much concentrated attention at first, the focus is only temporary. The real issue is a lifelong friendship with your wife that continues even after the children are gone.

When you welcome a new member to your growing family, other relationships are going to change, too. Here are some ways they can change for the better.

Your Parents

You will probably find your relationship with your parents changing now that you are a parent, too. Having a child gives you an opportunity to reflect on what your own folks went through. At times, the responsibility of parenthood must have been just as overwhelming for them. This time of reflection can create a new empathy with grandparents and bring about a healing process that can resolve past misunderstandings. Refuse to dwell on past hurts. Forgiving your parents' perceived mistakes is the first step in building a bridge between generations. Here are some specific things you can do to build that bridge:

• Recognize the unique heritage of your family. Recall family traditions and special times, and works to establish traditions for the new generation.

• Provide special times for grandparents and grandchildren to be together. Photograph or video them and other extended family members with your baby.

• Let grandparents be grandparents. This relationship is not the same as the parent-child relationship.

• Be flexible. There's nothing wrong with grandparents spoiling their grandchildren a little.

• If a grandparent is no longer living, show your children pictures and tell them stories about their family heritage.

Your Friends

Parenthood inevitably affects friendships. During the child-bearing years, it's common to feel a temporary alienation from friends. A new child means a period of adjustment, especially if it is the first, and time spent with friends will be reduced to a minimum. A true friend will understand this. On the other hand, you need to make sure that you continue to communicate with your friends. Call them once in a while, and e-mail them to let them know how much you value their friendship and appreciate their understanding.

Friendships are especially important for new mothers, and you need to encourage your wife to get out and nurture them, just as you need to take her away from her role as mother now and then to nurture her in her role as wife. Unless she has opportunities to communicate with other adults in similar circumstances, she will tend to unload all her frustration on you as soon as you walk in the door after a hard day's work.

If your wife gave up her job outside the home after the birth of your child, the transition may be difficult as she struggles to hold on to past relationships or seeks to make new friends with other mothers who choose to stay home with their children. She will benefit from getting together with other mothers for lunch at the park, bike rides, or trips to the zoo—activities for the children that also provide mothers with the opportunity to make new friends.

It might be difficult for your friends to understand why you can not "go out with the boys" as often, especially if they are not yet fathers or do not make their family a priority. Seek new friendships with those who have similar values, and strengthen old ties with those who are like-minded. Plan new activities that include the whole family. If your friends distance themselves as child-rearing differences emerge, it may be a blessing in disguise.

Your Baby's Siblings

As you focus on making the new addition a welcome member of the family, do not forget the existing member or members of the welcoming committee—the baby's siblings. Never underestimate how much a child is able to understand. If your life revolves around your children, the introduction of competition for your attention can devastate a sibling who had previously been given all the attention.

As the husband-wife relationship takes priority, the children see their places more clearly, and as they feel equally loved and accepted, the potential for jealousy fades. Here are several practical tips for helping prepare older children to accept their new sibling:

- If you plan to move an older child from a crib to a bed, do so at least one to two months before the baby's birth to allow the older child time to adjust.

- Talk about the baby's imminent arrival and what a great helper the older child can be.

- Either have potty training well under control or wait to begin until a few months after the baby's arrival.

- Allow older children to participate in the daily activities of the new baby. Include them when appropriate and when they express a desire to help. Even a two-year-old can feel very important when he holds and loves the new baby.

• Make a special time each day to focus on each child. Give them lots of hugs, kisses, and verbal affirmation, especially when the child exhibits a gentle, kind, and helpful spirit.

Your Baby

Now is the time to create special family memories and traditions. Take time each day to:

• Look into your child's face and learn his or her unique expressions.

• Sing songs and play games.

• Read books and tell him stories.

• Show your child how much you love each other as a husband and wife.

• Say "I love you."

• Give him a chance to appreciate his grandparents and other special family members.

• Enjoy the wonders of creation with him.

Changing Roles

Cultural changes have had a profound influence on how the roles of mother and father are viewed. One change that has taken place since mothers have entered the work force *en masse* is that it has become socially acceptable for the husband to assume a nurturing role. It's not at all unusual anymore to see a father changing a dirty diaper, folding laundry, fixing a meal, cleaning up in the kitchen after dinner, or helping out in a child's classroom at school. This is a positive change, because both parents should participate in training, nurturing, and disciplining the children. Children need to see the tender side of a loving father as he attends to their emotional as well as physical needs.

The trend has also been for both parents to pursue careers and leave the training and nurturing of their children to others. For many families it is economically necessary for a mother to work full-time outside the home. Yet it is a heavy burden for any mother to bear. To make a wise decision about whether both of you should work full-time outside the home, you should ask yourself these questions:

• Is our family a main priority in life?

• Are social status, personal convenience, and material possessions more important than time spent with family?

• Will we be able to look back on these years without regret?

• What kind of memories are we building?

• Are the special relationships of grandma/grandpa or aunt/uncle being compromised by having our extended family care for our children on a regular basis?

• Is our home being maintained while we both work full time?

- Who is taking responsibility for the spiritual upbringing of our children?

Beyond Becoming Birthwise

There are seasons of parenting. Beyond the birth experience awaits the stewardship of parenting. As you watch your baby's amazing growth in the first year of life, take time to reflect on the influence you will have on his character, for it is through the daily process of parenting that you instill values in your children.

A child who has been loved unconditionally can learn to give that same kind of love back. These days much emphasis is placed on building a child's self-esteem, yet feeling good about oneself really comes from doing what is right. Parents who strive to guide, encourage, and affirm their child while pointing him toward obedience—show him how to live a moral life. Parents who invest time in training their children to be still and quiet will reap the benefits by helping them develop a peaceful spirit.

Patience involves putting the need of others before your own. What a difficult thing for a toddler to learn! This does not happen overnight, but will over time, as you teach your child that the needs of others are as important as his and to wait patiently. Later in the child's life, as he practices patience with friends and learns to share, he will want to put another person's happiness before his own.

The home is the perfect place to model kindness. When kindness within all family relationships is taught and lived out, you don't need to expect or tolerate sibling rivalry. A child should learn to obey immediately the first time he is asked, without complaining. Praise and encouragement flow from the parent when a child chooses to obey.

Eventually, the child will make good choices on his own.

As parents, you have the job of teaching your child what it takes to be a faithful member of the family. This can start in the early months of the child's life through such things as cleaning up after playtime—even if he just picks up three toys. When the child is properly instructed, understands what he needs to do, and does it faithfully, he will know that he can be trusted with greater responsibilities.

Children need to be taught respect for everything around them—including nature, other people's property, authority figures, and peers. Treating these things with gentleness and respect is possible when the child learns to have self-control. The ability to control one's actions comes through discipline, which you can teach through the daily activities in a child's routine. A newborn will learn to trust that Mom and Dad will meet his physical needs when they are met with regularity. A crawling baby investigating his environment will learn to control his actions if parents give clear instructions, set boundaries, and stick to them.

During the early years, parents must establish their authority in their children's lives. If trust and respect for your authority is established in your child's early years, you will find the teen years can be quite enjoyable. The goal of the parent-child relationship is a mutual respect and love, in a friendship that comes to maturity in the late teen years. We encourage you to continue investing in, and reading the remaining books in the *"On Becoming"* series which gives detailed, practical advice for each phase of a child's life.

Epilogue

Parenting
in Process

They're on their own now. The new family settles in to the long-awaited lifestyle changes. The first day home the baby is so cute during the day, but will she also be so cute at a 3 A.M. feeding?

The parents recall what they learned in *On Becoming Babywise* about establishing order and routine in their lives. It sounded so easy in the book, but is the baby going to go along with their plan? "I never knew babies cried so much," sighs Dad. "I thought our baby would be different!" Mom exclaims. They begin to realize that this new chapter in their lives will be "parenting in process." They are learning how to anticipate what their baby needs and how to respond wisely.

Day-by-day the baby responds to the challenges asked of her. She is happy much of her awake time, but those times when she is fussy call for a parental pow-wow and common-sense answers. Guiding, anticipating, enjoying—Mom and Dad begin to see the delightful duty the stewardship of parenting is. The birth experience is now a treasured memory. Just as becoming *"birthwise"* helped them make all the decisions that had to be made at the beginning of their journey, so the road ahead will require the new parents to become wise about all the stages their daughter will pass through on her journey to adulthood.

A Timeline of Birth Practices

Seventeenth Century

• Care given by midwife, family, or women of community
• Natural remedies for support
• Birth at home

Eighteenth Century (Age of Enlightenment)

• Use of forceps

Nineteenth Century (Victorian Era)

• Use of chloroform
• Louis Pasteur identified microorganisms (1860)
• "Childbed fever" epidemic (1880s)
• Cesarean section revived (1882)
• Hospital seen as only for the poor and diseased (1890s)

Twentieth Century

1900–20s

• At the beginning of the last century, only 22 percent of babies were born in hospitals
• Professional standards and organizations established for health care
• Improved image for hospitals
• "Once a Cesarean Section, always a Cesarean Section" philosophy

- Medical personnel provide care
- Active management of labor: "twilight sleep" anesthesia
- Manual dilation of the cervix
- Routine episiotomy (an incision in the perineum to enlarge the vaginal opening)
- The practice of high forcep delivery
- By 1927, 76 percent of births occurred in hospitals
- Women in labor separated from family

1930s–40s

- Dr. Grantly Dick-Read wrote *"Childbirth Without Fear"*
- Birth is the ultimate feminine experience
- Birth not a fearful experience
- Labor companion (coach) encouraged
- Give in to labor, like waves flowing in and out

1950s

- "Baby boomer" mothers
- Bottle-feeding "in"
- La Leche League begun
- Heavily medicated labors and births
- Routine episiotomy and forceps delivery
- Lamaze method to decrease pain (1959)
- Fathers in labor room for support (but not in the delivery room)
- Breathing techniques used to avoid medication
- Fetal monitors introduced

1960s

- "The Pill"
- Dr. Bradley's idea of "husband-coached childbirth"
- Every woman is capable of natural childbirth
- Slow/deep breathing techniques
- Beware of medical procedures and intervention

1970s

- Bradley and Lamaze methods
- International Childbirth Education Association
  - Childbirth education classes
  - Increased practice of certified nurse-midwives
  - Heightened legal concerns at birth
- Natural childbirth
  - Breathing and relaxation techniques used to avoid medication
  - Alternate birth-center ("ABC" rooms)
  - Parent-infant bonding
- Routine episiotomy
- Increased number of Cesarean Sections
- *Roe v. Wade* legalizes abortion in America (1973)
- First test-tube baby born (1978)

1980s–90s

- Full-time working women
- Delayed child-bearing
- Sexual promiscuity
- Infertility
- Children in day-care

- AIDS
- Informed consent
- Birth plans
- Advanced technology
- Epidurals common
- Vaginal birth after Cesarean Section (VBAC)
- Family-centered maternity care
- Alternative births (freestanding birth-center, home birth, water birth)
- Avoidance of episiotomy and interventions
- In Vitro Fertilization

2000 and beyond

- Use of epidurals
- Induction of labor for convenience more common
- Cesarean Section by patient request
- Fewer VBACs; more repeat Cesarean Sections
- GIFT, ZIFT, surrogate motherhood
- Increasing numbers of premature births
- Delayed child-bearing and older first-time mothers
- More multiple births due to technological advances
- More advanced prenatal testing, including 4-D ultrasounds

Appendix B

Conception Prevention

Kind	How It Works	Effectiveness	Advantages	Disadvantages
Oral contraceptive pill	Contains estrogen and progesterone, which prevent ovulation, make the cervical mucus thicker, and alter the lining of the uterus	99%	• Simple and effective • Does not interfere with marital intimacy • Menstrual periods are regular, with less cramping	• Possible minor side effects include nausea, headaches, weight gain, irregular menstrual bleeding, increased blood pressure • Strokes and heart attacks are possible for women over 35 who smoke or have certain medical problems • Could decrease supply of breast milk • Blood clots in lungs or legs (rare)
Contraceptive patch	Similar to oral contraceptives, but worn as a patch that releases hormones continuously	99%	• Similar to oral contraceptives, but no need to remember to take a pill every day	• Similar to oral contraceptives • Difficulty with patch adhering
Contraceptive vaginal ring	Similar to oral contraceptives A ring placed inside the vagina for 3 weeks releases hormones continuously; removed for 1 week to allow for a period	99%	• Similar to oral contraceptives, but no need to remember to take a pill every day	• Similar to oral contraceptives • Difficulty with insertion and removal

Kind	How It Works	Effectiveness	Advantages	Disadvantages
Minipill	Contains progesterone, which prevents ovulation, makes the cervical mucus thicker, and alters the lining of the uterus	95%	• Simple and effective • Does not interfere with marital intimacy • Can be used while breast-feeding • Fewer side effects than regular oral contraceptive pill	• Less effective if not taken consistently • Irregular vaginal bleeding or missed menstrual periods • Can induce an abortion
Intrauterine device (IUD)	• Small plastic, copper-wrapped device inserted in the uterus creates an inflammatory reaction that is toxic to sperm and eggs; secondarily, prevents the implantation of a fertilized egg • Progesterone-containing IUD has a more pronounced effect on the lining of the uterus to prevent implantation	97%	• Effective • Replaced every 10 years • Progesterone IUD replaced every 5 years; menstrual bleeding decreased or absent	• Must be inserted by doctor • Risks with insertion: pelvic infection, uterine perforation • Uterus may expel the device • Increased menstrual bleeding and cramping with copper IUD • Not as effective in preventing tubal pregnancy • Could induce an abortion
Diaphragm	Rubber cup with spermicide is inserted into the vagina prior to marital intimacy to create a barrier between the uterus and sperm and hold the spermicide against the cervix	90%	Safe and inexpensive	• Must be fitted by doctor, particularly postpartum and if there has been a weight change of more than 15 pounds • Requires insertion prior to marital intimacy • Use with spermicide increases the possibility of urinary tract infections or vaginal irritation

Kind	How It Works	Effectiveness	Advantages	Disadvantages
Condom	A rubber sheath placed over the penis to prevent sperm from reaching the uterus	• 88% alone • 94% with spermicide in the vagina	• Safe • Provides protection against sexually transmitted infections	• May interfere with marital intimacy • May break • May decrease sensation for the man
Spermicide	Prior to marital intimacy a cream, gel, or suppository is inserted in the vagina with or without a diaphragm	85%	Safe	• Messy • Can cause vaginal irritation
Cervical cap (used with spermicide)	Creates a barrier between the uterus and sperm and kills the sperm	82%	• Safe • Can be inserted several hours prior to marital intimacy • May be more comfortable than a diaphragm	• Must be fitted by doctor • May be difficult to insert • Must be left in place for 8 hours after marital intimacy
Subdermal implants (Norplant)	6 capsules are inserted under the skin in the upper arm to releases progesterone, which prevents ovulation, makes the cervical mucus thicker, and alters the lining of the uterus	99%	• Effective • Replaced every 5 years	• Expensive • Needs to be surgically inserted and removed using local anesthesia • Causes irregular or missed menstrual periods • May cause an abortion
Injectable contraceptive Depo-provera (progesterone only) Lonelle (estrogen and progesterone)	Given by injection every 3 months to inhibit ovulation Given by injection every month	99%	• Effective • Can be used while breastfeeding • Similar to oral contraceptives, but no need to remember to take a pill every day	• Irregular or absent menstrual periods • Possible side effects: mood swings, weight gain

Kind	How It Works	Effectiveness	Advantages	Disadvantages
Natural family planning	Marital intimacy is avoided at the woman's fertile time of month as determined by basal body temperature, changes in cervical mucus, and length of menstrual cycles	80%	• Safe • Improves body awareness	• Requires understanding and discipline to carry out properly • Requires 10 to 14 days of abstinence per month • Difficult to use when breastfeeding or when menstrual cycles are irregular
Sterilization	Surgical interruption of fallopian tubes (tubal ligation) or of the ducts carrying sperm (vasectomy)	99%	Permanent and effective	• Not usually reversible • Requires surgical procedure with general anesthetic for a tubal ligation and local anesthetic for a vasectomy • Complications from surgery (rare)

Labor Variations and Options
(See Chapter Two)

Medications and Anesthesia

Medications to Increase Comfort During Labor

What is it?	What does it do?	When is it given?	How is it given?	Are there risks or side effects?
Sedatives • Nembutal • Ambien • Restoril	• Allows mother to rest • Helps relieve anxiety	• During the early phase of labor • With prolonged labor	• Orally • Possibly IM	*Mother* • May slow labor • May increase drowsiness *Baby* • May accumulate in tissues • May affect initial responsiveness and ability to suck
Tranquilizers • Vistaril • Phenergan • Compazine	• Used to relieve tension and anxiety • May control nausea • Will enhance the effect when given with analgesics	Anytime during labor	• IM • IV	*Mother* • Dry mouth • Drowsiness *Baby* • Variation of heart rate • May affect initial muscle tone and ability to suck after birth
Analgesics • Demerol • Morphine • Stadol • Fentanyl	• Used to reduce or alter perception of pain without loss of consciousness • Demerol may relax cervix and hasten dilation	During active labor	• IM • IV	*Mother* • Dizziness • Nausea • Difficulty concentrating • Usually needs more active support from coach *Baby* • Depressed respiration if given too close to delivery or too frequently

What is it?	What does it do?	When is it given?	How is it given?	Are there risks or side effects?
Oxytocics • Oxytocin • Pitocin	Used to stimulate contractions and induce labor	• During labor to enhance contractions • After delivery to reduce postpartum bleeding	• IV • IM • Natural release of oxytocin with breast pump or nipple stimulation	*Mother* • More frequent contractions that peak faster • Increased desire for pain medication • Increased need for coaching and support *Baby* • Variations in heart rate
Prostaglandins • Cervidil • Misoprostol (cytotec)	Softens cervix to make induction easier	Same as above	• Prostaglandin through vaginal gel or suppository • Ribbon placed behind cervix	Same as above
Labor inhibitors • Terbutaline • Magnesium sulfate • Ritodrine • Procardia • Indomethacin	Used to stop premature labor	Possibility of premature labor when contractions are present before 36 weeks	• Orally • Continuous subcutaneous infusion • IV or IM with simultaneous fetal and uterine monitoring • May be given subcutaneously on an outpatient basis for prolonged suppression of premature labor	*Mother* • Increased heart rate • Palpitations • Headache • Nervousness • Trembling *Baby* • Variations in heart rate • Decreased blood sugar at birth

Anesthesia Used for Labor and Delivery

What is it?	What is its effect or advantage?	When and how is it administered?	What are the risks and side effects?
Local infiltration	• Numbs the perineum in preparation for an episiotomy or for repair of the incision or any tears • Takes effect in 3 to 4 minutes and lasts approximately 30 minutes	Injected into the perineum just prior to the birth of the baby or after delivery for repair	*Mother* May feel burning or stinging sensation when it is administered *Baby* None
Epidural block	• Loss of sensation from waist to toes, usually providing complete relief of pain from contractions, birth, and repairs • Lasts about 1 1/2 to 2 hours after the anesthetic has been discontinued	• During active labor, the second stage of labor, or before a C-section • Introduced into the epidural space at the level of the lower lumbar vertebrae • A thin tube is inserted and remains in place throughout labor for continuous administration of the anesthetic • Some hospitals offer a "walking" epidural, which allows more mobility but provides less pain relief	*Mother* • Decreased ability to move and loss of sensation from the waist to the toes • Prolonged labor • Lower blood pressure • Less urge to push • More need for forceps delivery and medical intervention (IV, Pitocin, fetal monitor) • Possible headache *Baby* • Decreased oxygen intake with decreased maternal blood pressure • Decreased heart rate
Spinal	• Loss of sensation from breast to toes • Lasts 30 minutes to 3 hours, depending on the agent used	• Given prior to a C-section • Introduced by passing a needle through the lumbar vertebrae and injecting the medication into the spinal canal	*Mother* Complete paralysis of the lower torso and legs *Baby* None
General	The patient is asleep, and breathing is assisted throughout the procedure	• IV and inhalation of gases • Used when the baby has to be delivered immediately or if maternal medical conditions contraindicate the use of an epidural or spinal anesthesia	*Mother* • Possible aspiration of stomach contents, causing pneumonia *Baby* • May inhibit the ability to initiate breathing after delivery

Postpartum Medication

What is it?	What is its effect?	When is it administered	How is it administered	What are the risks and side effects?
Analgesic • Tylenol with codeine • Darvocet • Percodan • Percocet • Ibuprofen • Vicodan	• Relieves pain • Ibuprofen decreases swelling • Useful in providing the comfort and relaxation needed for optimum breast-feeding	Usually given as needed for relief of episiotomy discomfort and cramping after birth	Orally	*Mother* • Drowsiness • Constipation *Baby* Minimal amounts may be present in breast milk
Analgesic • Dura-morph	• Relieves pain after a C-section • Provides complete relief for 12 to 24 hours	Given at the completion of a C-section prior to transfer to recovery room	Administered through the same catheter used for epidural or with spinal	• Itching • Respiratory depression • Nausea and vomiting
Stool softener • DOSS • Pericolace • Metamucil	Softens stools to prevent straining while the perineum heals	Once a day for 1 to 2 weeks after birth	Orally (mother should drink lots of liquids)	May want to use natural remedies
• Methergine • Oxytocin • Prostglandins	• Stimulates contraction of the uterus • Helps decrease bleeding	• 3 times a day for 2 days • Given only as needed for excessive vaginal bleeding or a boggy uterus	• Orally • IM • IV	Painful uterine contractions

Procedures, Options and Variations

Common Procedures and Options

Option	Purpose	Disadvantages	Alternative
Enema	• To provide more room for the baby's descent • To avoid the release of bowels during the second stage of labor • To reduce the possibility of postpartum constipation		• Self-administer in hospital • Use of small-volume enema (Fleet) • No enema • Rarely done anymore unless the patient requests it
Intravenous fluids (IV) Flexible catheter is inserted into a vein for the continuous administration of fluids	• To maintain an adequate fluid balance and prevent dehydration during prolonged labor • To provide access for direct administration of medications if needed during labor and delivery, or if there is an emergency	Mobility may be restricted	• Increase oral intake of fluids • Have an IV inserted and capped, to be used only when needed (heparin lock)
External uterine contraction monitor 2 belts are placed around the abdomen	• To assess frequency, quality, and duration of contractions • To monitor the relationship of contractions to the fetal heart rate	Restriction of mobility	• Intermittently monitor the baby's heart with a stethoscope in a low-risk delivery • No monitoring if fetal well-being is established
Internal fetal monitor • Wire is inserted into the vagina and attached to the baby's scalp • A second tube may be inserted into the uterus to monitor uterine contractions	To accurately assess fetal well-being	• Local scalp irritation or infection in the newborn • Restricted movement of mother • Risk of infection • Rupture of membranes is required for placement of an internal monitor	• Use external monitor • Use only in case of significant meconium in the amniotic fluid, abnormal fetal heart rate, fetal distress, or inability to assess fetal heart rate externally

Option	Purpose	Disadvantages	Alternative
Intrauterine pressure catheter	To accurately assess the strength and frequency of uterine contractions in the presence of abnormal labor, Pitocin-enhanced labor, an abnormal fetal heart rate, or a previous C-section	• Uterine infection • Injury to the uterus, placenta, or baby • Increased vaginal bleeding • Restricted movement of the mother	Use external uterine contraction monitor
Bedrest	• To provide rest during labor • To correct or stabilize maternal or fetal vital signs • To allow for continuous fetal and uterine monitoring • To decrease the chance of prolapsed umbilical cord if the presenting part is not engaged in the pelvis and the membranes have ruptured		• Continue walking and other activity, as tolerated • May be permitted to walk after membranes have ruptured if the baby's head is well engaged in the pelvis
Restricted oral intake	• To decrease the chance of aspiration (breathing vomit into the lungs) early in labor if general anesthesia is needed for surgical procedures • To decrease nausea and vomiting from slowed digestion during labor		• Eat light, easily digested foods, as tolerated • Drink clear liquids to provide hydration • Use intravenous fluids to maintain hydration
Artificial rupture of membranes (AROM)	• To see if meconium is present in the amniotic fluid • To improve uterine contractions and accelerate labor • To allow for placement of internal monitors • May be performed in active labor if spontaneous rupture has not occurred	• Increased incident of infection and prolapsed umbilical cord if the baby's head is not well engaged • May not improve the uterine contraction pattern • May commit to delivery within a certain number of hours, depending on the policies of the delivering facility	Wait for spontaneous rupture of the membranes

Option	Purpose	Disadvantages	Alternative
Vaginal (cervical) examinations	• To identify the progress of cervical changes in labor • To identify or confirm the presenting part of the baby	Increased incidence of infection in the presence of ruptured membranes	Limit the number of examinations
Pain medication	• To promote relaxation during labor • To allow labor to progress by eliminating hindrances caused by pain	• May slow labor if given too early • Maternal drowsiness	• Walk to provide distraction • Change position often • Use breathing and relaxation techniques • Have a massage • Take a warm shower or bath (in the absence of risk) • Use a heating pad or warm compresses • Implement PURE
Episiotomy Doctor makes an incision from the vaginal opening toward the rectum	• To decrease the possibility of extensive perineal tears • To minimize pressure on the baby's head • To facilitate progress of the second stage of labor • To allow access for delivery by forceps or vacuum extractor delivery • To expedite delivery if there are complications	• Further extension of the incision by tearing • Increased bleeding from the incision • Infection at incision site • Postpartum perineal discomfort • Increased fear of resuming sexual intimacy after delivery • Scar tissue	• Communicate well with doctor during the pushing stage • Push slowly at end-stage • Apply warm packs to the perineum • Lubricate the vagina with mineral oil, lubricating jelly, or water during the pushing stage • Massage and gently stretch the vaginal and perineal tissue • Deliver in a side-lying position

Option	Purpose	Disadvantages	Alternative
Stirrups	To separate and support the legs for easy viewing and access to the perineum	• Possible damage to the nerves behind the knee if the stirrups are used for a prolonged period • Increased incidence of leg cramps	• Place feet on the bed during pushing and delivery • If perineal repair is indicated, use foot support stirrups instead • May be necessary with an epidural if the mother is unable to move her legs
Sterile drapes	To provide a sterile area for delivery of the baby and surgical repair of an episiotomy and lacerations		Use only if repair is needed
Lights	To allow the doctor to see the perineum and the baby during delivery		• Turn off the overhead lights and use a spotlight on the perineum • During the day, use natural lighting • Dim the lights
Cutting the umbilical cord	To separate the mother and baby after delivery • Immediate: right after birth • Delayed: after pulsation in the cord stops	Delay may negatively affect the baby's blood volume	• In the absence of meconium, wait to cut the cord until the baby takes a deep breath or lets out a hearty cry • Have a family participant cut the cord
Prophylactic (preventive) treatment of the eyes of the newborn	To decrease or eliminate the risk of eye infection from vaginal secretions infected by sexually transmitted diseases (gonorrhea and chlamydia)		This treatment, required by federal law, may be waived with parental consent in the absence of risk from sexually transmitted diseases
Transporting newborn to the hospital nursery	• To stabilize the baby • To provide routine care for the baby		If no complications exist, deliver in an environment where the newborn is not removed from the parents after birth and where care is given in their presence

Option	Purpose	Disadvantages	Alternative
Bathe newborn in the hospital nursery	To relax the baby and promote alertness		A family member may give the bath within the first few hours of birth
Breast-feeding	• To provide nourishment for the newborn • To help the uterus contract after delivery		Bottle-feeding

Possible Variations in Labor

Type	Definition	Signs/Symptoms	Intervention	Risk/Benefit
Precipitous labor	Labor that lasts 3 hours or less from onset to delivery	• The onset of labor is very intense and may be interpreted as early difficult labor • Mother has difficulty relaxing during intense contractions	• Use of relaxation and breathing techniques to cope with the contractions • Good coaching to provide support and encouragement	Labor may progress so quickly that the baby may be born before help is obtained
Prolonged (prodromal) labor	Labor that lasts at least 24 hours before delivery perhaps due to: • Ineffective contractions • Malposition • Posterior position of baby • Large baby/small pelvis • Extreme tension • Maternal malnutrition or dehydration • Medications given during labor • Premature use of anesthesia	Contractions may be regular or irregular with increased periods of rest between them	• Rest • Encouragement • Relaxing environment • Walk to increase frequency and intensity of contractions • Pitocin by IV, or nipple stimulation to help strengthen contractions • Intravenous fluids for maternal hydration and nutrition • Sedative to provide rest	• Increased chance of infection if membranes have been ruptured for a prolonged period • Increased incidence of C-section

Type	Definition	Signs/Symptoms	Intervention	Risk/Benefit
Back labor (experienced by 1 in 4 women)	Labor that is felt mostly in the lower back perhaps due to: • Posterior position of the baby • Breech presentation • Extreme tension • Variations in maternal anatomy • Remaining in back-lying position during labor	May be more difficult to relax with contractions	To move the baby into an anterior position: • Change position frequently • Lie on back with a rolled blanket under the small of the back • Increase the angle of the spine to make the baby uncomfortable so he will change position. • Use side-lying position with pillows supporting the head and abdomen and between the legs • Alternate side-lying positions every 15 minutes until the baby's rotation is complete Comfort measures: • Do not labor in back-lying position • Sit on a chair backward, leaning forward onto the back of the chair for support • Sit in Tailor position • Do the pelvic rock exercise between contractions • Apply counterpressure to the lower back during the contraction • Massage or apply heat to lower back	Increased need for medical intervention (forceps, vacuum extractor, episiotomy, C-section)

Possible Interventions

Fetal Distress

Intervention	Reason for It	Description	Risk/Disadvantage
Amnioinfusion	• To dilute thick meconium-stained amniotic fluid • To avoid meconium aspiration syndrome • To increase volume of amniotic fluid • To decrease umbilical cord compression	Warm saline is slowly instilled from an IV bag through an intrauterine pressure catheter during labor	• Membranes must be ruptured • Over distention of the uterus • Infection
Oxygen	• To increase the level of oxygen in the mother's blood • To improve the amount of oxygen delivered to the baby	Humidified oxygen delivered by mask or nasal prongs	

Prolonged or Ineffective Labor

Intervention	Reason for It	Description	Risk/Disadvantage
Stripping of the membranes	To induce labor	The doctor may cause release of prostaglandins by inserting fingers between the dilated cervix and the amniotic sac to loosen the sac from the uterine wall	• Infection • May not initiate labor if done too soon • Can be uncomfortable for the mother
Amniotomy (Artificial rupture of the membranes)	• Induce labor • Allow positioning of interior monitors • Increase quality and intensity of contractions	A long, crochet hook–like instrument inserted through the vagina and cervix to tear the amniotic membranes	• Infection • Prolapsed cord if presenting part is not engaged in the pelvis • Tends to commit to delivery within a specified time, depending on the delivering facility

Intervention	Reason for It	Description	Risk/Disadvantage
Administering oxytocin or Pitocin	• Induce labor • Enhance contractions	• Given intravenously • Contractions are more frequent, last longer, and peak quickly • More intense and uncomfortable contractions	• Fetal distress • Internal monitoring is usually required

Difficulties With the Baby Passing Through the Birth Canal

Intervention	Reason for It	Description	Risk/Disadvantage
Forceps	To help pull the baby from the birth canal	Forceps are inserted into the vagina and placed on either side of the baby's head	• May require anesthesia • May require an episiotomy • May cause vaginal lacerations • May bruise the baby's face • May cause facial nerve damage to the baby (rare)
Vacuum extractor	• To help the baby move down the birth canal • To assist the mother in pushing effectively	A caplike suction device is placed on a portion of the baby's head, and the doctor adjusts the amount of suction	• Swelling on the soft tissue of the baby's scalp, which may take several days to go down • A lump or swelling on the baby's head that is filled with blood (cephalohematoma) and may take weeks to be absorbed • Requires an episiotomy • May cause brain damage if used for an extended period of time

The Stages of Labor

(See Chapter Five)

First Stage of Labor: Early Phase

Physical/Emotional Symptoms	Actions to Take	Comfort Measures	Coach's Role
Contractions* • Felt as menstrual cramps, intestinal gas pains, lower backache, pelvic pressure, discomfort in groin or upper-thigh area • May be mild, irregular	• Assess and time contractions • Change position and assess them again • Maintain relaxed breathing pattern • Use cleansing breath before and after each contraction • Use relaxation techniques • Urinate frequently • Conserve energy • Call doctor as prearranged	• Use relaxation techniques • Except for cleansing breaths, use breathing techniques only if necessary • Do the pelvic rock exercise to ease lower-back discomfort • Take a warm shower • Lightly massage your abdomen (effleurage)	• Monitor contractions • Continue "life as usual" until they become more intense • If contractions begin at night, encourage the mother to sleep • Facilitate PURE • Time contractions • Eat a good meal and prepare snacks ahead • Make sure suitcases and supplies are ready • Make arrangements for other children • Drive carefully to the medical facility • Review labor flowchart
Flu-like symptoms: loose bowel movements, nausea, achiness	If doctor agrees, drink clear liquids and eat light foods (Jell-O, soda, soup, tea)		Encourage fluid intake
Feeling excited, relieved, nervous, apprehensive, talkative, and impatient	Share feelings with coach		• Encourage expression of feelings • Share excitement

*Note: Contractions may decrease in frequency or even stop after you're admitted to a medical facility. This is caused by the release of adrenaline, which can directly affect the uterus.

First Stage of Labor: Active Phase

Physical/Emotional Symptoms	Actions to Take	Comfort Measures	Coach's Role
Contractions • Stronger, regular, frequent, build to a peak more rapidly, and last longer • May be more intense during a vaginal exam • May be strong in the lower back if the baby is in a posterior position Feelings • May feel tense, preoccupied, serious, discouraged, less talkative, concerned about ability to cope with contractions • Unable to find a comfortable position or express her needs and desires	• Change positions often • Urinate every hour • Ask about dilation, effacement, station, and position of baby when checked vaginally by the doctor	• Use relaxation techniques and breathing techniques if necessary • Massage the abdomen • Implement PURE • Concentrate on one contraction at a time • Relax completely between contractions • Apply counterpressure on lower back, sit in a rocking chair, shower if possible • Use medication if desired	• Time contractions • Offer continuous encouragement, praise, and companionship • Offer ice chips, lip balm • Monitor for signs of hyperventilation • Encourage a slow breathing pattern • Massage tense areas as desired • Massage lower back to relieve discomfort
May have nausea and vomiting	• Slow, deep breathing between contractions • Rest between contractions	• Ice chips • Cool washcloth to face and neck	• View events as positive indicator that labor is progressing • Give encouragement • Watch for signs of hyperventilation

First Stage of Labor: Transition

Physical/Emotional Symptoms	Actions to Take	Comfort Measures	Coach's Role
Contraction • Very strong, very long in duration, peak almost immediately • May have double contractions or multiple peaks within each contraction • May perceive contractions as continuous	• Use relaxation techniques • Use breathing technique that best allows coping with the contractions • Take one contraction at a time, and rest between them • Change positions, if desired	• Use back massage and counterpressure to lower back • Shower, if able • Walk • Sit in a rocking chair	• Give her continuous praise and encouragement • Talk her through each contraction, if needed • Breathe with her to help her maintain a slow, controlled breathing pattern • Apply cool washcloth to her face, forehead, or neck, if desired • Apply warm washcloth to perineum to aid in relaxation • Encourage her to urinate every 30 minutes to an hour • Encourage position changes
Premature urge to push	• Candle-blow through contraction • Do not push unless instructed by doctor	Use appropriate breathing techniques	• Notify doctor if urge to push is present • Strongly assist her in candle-blow breathing • Encourage her not to push
Trembling in legs or leg cramps	Hyperextend the heel of the affected leg and point toes toward ceiling	Warm blankets, if desired	• Encourage her to change position • Apply counterpressure to affected leg, pointing toes upward toward head
Nausea and vomiting	Take slow, deep breaths between contractions	• Slow, deep breathing • Ice chips	• Encourage her that labor is progressing • Remind her that transition is the shortest stage of labor

Physical/Emotional Symptoms	Actions to Take	Comfort Measures	Coach's Role
Discomfort in lower back, buttocks, groin, perineum		• Change position • Apply counterpressure to lower back • Apply warm compresses to perineum	• Apply counterpressure to her lower back, if desired • Offer to massage her back • Encourage her to change position
Dry mouth from breathing through the mouth during contractions	Breathe with tongue behind upper teeth	• Ice chips • Rinse mouth with water or mouthwash	Offer her ice chips, mouthwash, lip balm
Hot or cold sensation		• Blankets • Cool washcloth	• Offer blankets if she's cold • Offer cool washcloth or ice chips if she's warm
Introverted (unable to communicate with others), anxious, frightened at loss of control, panicked (does not feel she can endure more labor), discouraged, irritable, confused, forgetful, disoriented	Take one contraction at a time	• Use relaxation techniques • Use the breathing techniques most effective in helping you cope with contractions	• Continue to encourage her that labor is progressing • Be supportive and firm • Do not be overly sensitive to her response • Accept her irritability and praise her efforts • Be sensitive to her pain • Orient her to her surroundings if she is confused • Breathe with her, if needed • *Do not* leave her during this stage

Second Stage of Labor: Pushing and Birth

Physical/Emotional Symptoms	Actions to Take	Comfort Measures	Coach's Role
Powerful, expulsive contractions with longer intervals between them			Remind her that longer intervals between contractions is normal during this stage
Irresistible urge to push, typically described as the need to have a bowel movement (some women do not feel this urge)	• Get into position desired for pushing (see p. 73) • With the urge, push at the peak of the contraction • If instructed not to push, use candle-blow breathing until contraction is over or the urge to push passes • Rest completely between contractions • Avoid holding breath • Relax perineum	• Take a cleansing breath before and after each contraction • Control the release of breath throughout the pushing • Hold your breath for a count of 10 during active pushing, repeating throughout the contraction	• Notify her doctor when she begins to feel the urge to push • Help her get into the desired position for pushing • Decide if she needs you to count out loud or just give her silent support during pushing • Help her candle-blow breathe
• Bulging of the rectum and perineum • Possible increase of blood from vagina, urine leakage, and passing of amniotic fluid	Relax perineum as much as possible	Use warm washcloth on perineum, if desired	Encourage her that this signals the baby's descent through the birth canal
Crowning of the baby's head at the vaginal opening	Notify doctor if he is not in the room		Birth is imminent
Stretching, bulging, or splitting sensation as the baby's head stretches the perineal tissues	• Follow doctor's instructions about when and how to push • If progress is slow, change pushing position	Try to push through the discomfort until the pressure of the baby's head provides natural anesthetic effect	• Help her to push or not to push, as instructed • Encourage her to continue to push through the discomfort • Position a mirror so she can see the baby's progress • If progress is slow, help her change her pushing position

Physical/Emotional Symptoms	Actions to Take	Comfort Measures	Coach's Role
• Renewal of energy, determination, and excitement • Relieved, but fearful of contractions • Talkative between contractions	May take several contractions before an adequate pushing technique is established	Assume position of comfort	• Encourage her through each contraction • Help her get into the best position for pushing • Share in the excitement of the impending birth
Episiotomy, if needed	• Doctor may administer anesthesia prior to performing the episiotomy • Follow doctor's instructions		Encourage relaxed breathing
Birth of the baby		• Use breathing techniques, if necessary • Relax as much as possible	Help her follow instructions during the birth
• Expressions of joy, awe, relief, gratitude, and disbelief • May cry or laugh uncontrollably • Concern shifts to baby	• Touch, hold, caress your newborn • Breastfeed immediately, if desired and possible • Talk to your baby		• Share the joy • Touch, hold, and talk to the baby • Take pictures

Third Stage of Labor: Separation of the Placenta

Physical/Emotional Symptoms	Actions to Take	Comfort Measures	Coach's Role
Contractions cease immediately after birth, then resume briefly to expel the placenta (many women do not experience discomfort during this stage and are unaware of the expulsion of the placenta)	• Use relaxation and breathing techniques, if necessary • Follow instructions to push, if necessary	Place baby to breast to encourage the release of oxytocin, which will aid in the expulsion of the placenta	• Share in the joy of the birth of the baby • Encourage relaxation and cooperation
There may be a rise in the abdomen, a lengthening of the umbilical cord, and an increase in blood from the vagina, which indicate that the placenta has separated	Follow doctor's instructions	Relax and use breathing techniques	Encourage relaxation and the use of breathing techniques

Care of the Mother After Delivery

Physical/Emotional Symptoms	Actions to Take	Comfort Measures	Coach's Role
• Doctor may order an injection of Pitocin, or it may be added to the IV fluid to help the uterus contract • Additional medication such as Methergine may be given if the uterus is slow to firm up after an injection of Pitocin			Encourage her by reminding her what she has done
Uterus may be very sensitive and tender	Uterus will be massaged externally to stimulate contraction and decrease vaginal bleeding	• Use breathing and relaxation techniques as necessary • Ask the doctor to show you how to massage the uterus effectively	• Encourage her to relax • Assist her as necessary
If repairing the perineum is necessary, it may cause pain	• Tell doctor if it is painful • Relax	• Use breathing and relaxation techniques, as necessary • Ask for an ice pack to decrease swelling and discomfort at repair site during recovery	• Encourage her to relax • Be supportive
May have chills or trembling	• Ask for warm blankets, orange juice, or other beverage to increase your blood sugar level • Use deep, slow breathing technique	• Try to relax muscles • Do not attempt to stop trembling • Use warm blankets	• Encourage her to rest, drink fluids, and eat some food • Encourage her to take slow, deep breaths
Doctor will monitor blood pressure, pulse, temperature, respiration, contraction of the uterus, and the amount of vaginal bleeding			Share the joy of having a new baby

Appendix E

Cesarean Section
(See Chapter Six)

Condition	Risk in Vaginal Delivery	Can C-Section Be Avoided?	How to Avoid	Risk/Alternative
Abnormal position • Breech (feet or buttocks first) • Transverse (lying on side) • Abnormal head position (face presentation)	• Cord accident • Aspiration of amniotic fluid • Fetal distress • Stillbirth • Cervix closing around the baby's neck before the head is delivered	• Yes, if the baby's position can be changed • Vaginal delivery possible only by obstetrician with experience in breech deliveries	External version (Using ultrasound and possibly medications to relax the uterus, the baby is repositioned by external, manual manipulation.)	C-section in case of: • Placental abruption • Entanglement of umbilical cord • Baby returns to former position • Fetal distress
Fetal distress	• Lack of blood and oxygen to the brain, which may lead to brain damage • Stillbirth	Yes, if distress is temporary	• Change mother's position • Give oxygen • Increase IV fluids • Exam vaginally to assess possible cord prolapse • Lift baby's head vaginally to reduce pressure of cord • Discontinue use of Pitocin • Assess baby's recovery from distress episodes	Emergency C-section if signs of distress persist (rapid vaginal delivery by maternal pushing or use of forceps or vacuum may be considered)

Condition	Risk in Vaginal Delivery	Can C-Section Be Avoided?	How to Avoid	Risk/Alternative
Maternal medical conditions • Diabetes • Cardiac disease • Active genital herpes • Rh sensitization	Depends on severity of the condition	Yes	Induction of labor by Pitocin may be possible for vaginal delivery	C-section if the situation demands
Pregnancy-induced hypertension (toxemia)	Maternal convulsions may cause stillbirth due to decreased blood and oxygen flow to the baby	Depends on the severity of the condition	Induction of labor by Pitocin may be possible for vaginal delivery	C-section if the situation demands
Ineffective contractions	• Maternal exhaustion • Fetal distress	Depends on the severity of the condition	• Empty bladder • Give Pitocin to augment contractions • Give medications to help mother relax • Change activity or position	C-section if progress is not evident after intervention or if fetal distress occurs
Placenta previa (placenta partially or completely covering the cervix)	• Maternal hemorrhage • Delivery of the placenta prior to the baby, causing death of baby or mother	• Unlikely except with partial previa • Not possible with complete previa	• Delivery room may be set up for a C-section and vaginal delivery • Speculum exam is performed once the cervix is dilated	If bleeding occurs, a C-section will be performed immediately

Condition	Risk in Vaginal Delivery	Can C-Section Be Avoided?	How to Avoid	Risk/Alternative
Placental abruption • May be partial or complete • Signs/symptoms: sharp abdominal pain, dark or bright red vaginal bleeding	Death of mother and baby	Occasionally, if labor is progressing quickly, bleeding is not excessive, and there is no evidence of fetal distress		
Cephalopelvic disproportion (CPD) May be caused by: • Size of the mother's pelvis • Size of the baby • Position of the baby's head	• Extended labor • Extensive tearing of perineum • Molding of the baby's head • Serious injury to the baby (fracture of the clavicle, dislocation of the shoulder) • Nerve injury • Death of the baby	Depends on the reason for CPD		
Cord accidents • Prolapsed cord • Knotted cord • Cord wrapped around baby's neck, causing fetal distress*	• Death of the baby • Neurological damage from decreased oxygen to the baby's brain during labor and delivery	Sometimes, if vaginal delivery is imminent		
Previous cesarean delivery (VBAC)	Depends on the reason for the previous C-section	Yes, if there has been only 1 prior C-section with a lower transverse incision	Anticipate vaginal delivery unless a need arises to indicate a C-section	

*Many cord accidents are not identified until after the birth of the baby. Also, in approximately 25 percent of all vaginal births, the cord is wrapped around the baby's neck but doesn't cause any complications.

Appendix F

Meeting Postpartum Challenges
(See Chapter Eight)

Problem	Practical Solution
Previous conditions • You have a medical problem that could have been affected by hormonal changes during pregnancy • You have a history of unresolved emotional depression unrelated to pregnancy	• Seek professional help in uncovering the nature of the problem • Anticipate potential emotional changes • Communicate your feelings to your spouse and discuss the practical aspects of postpartum care with him
Lack of sleep • You aren't getting enough sleep while adjusting to your new baby and his feeding schedule • You aren't getting enough sleep due to physical causes	• Recognize that a period of adjustment is necessary • Establish a parent-directed feeding plan • Try to nap when the baby sleeps • Take appropriate measures to relieve pain • Recognize that hormonal changes are temporary • Maintain a bedtime ritual • If you're unable to go back to sleep when awakened in the night, seek advice from your doctor
Pregnancy wasn't planned	• Discuss your concerns with your spouse and other family members as appropriate • Think creatively about how to address areas of difficulty such as lack of space
Difficult recovery	• Discuss the problems with your spouse • Seek accurate information from your doctor to help resolve the difficulties
Unexpected outcomes • Baby is born premature, ill, handicapped, or dead • The baby is of a different sex or appearance than anticipated	• List the practical concerns associated with the outcomes • Discuss your disappointments openly with your spouse • Seek support and encouragement from couples in similar circumstances • Reflect on the positive aspects of the outcome

Problem	Practical Solution
Fear	
• You're afraid you aren't adequate for the task of parenting a newborn	• Communicate your feelings openly • Seek advice from other parents • Attend parenting classes • Set realistic goals
• You're afraid harm will come to your baby	• Seek information about realistic areas of concern (e.g., SIDS) and what can be done to prevent problems
• You're afraid of changing the existing family dynamics	• If you are adding your first child, discuss the ramifications for your relationship as a couple • If you are adding another child, encourage each family member to be part of a team
• You fear that life is getting out of control because you feel you have too much responsibility	• Set up a daily schedule • Identify areas of concern and create a plan of action • Revise your expectations • Aim to provide a simple, tranquil home environment
Significant change in circumstances	
• Stressful events like death in the family or moving to a new area	• Maintain contact with familiar support people • Establish new routines while continuing some familiar traditions • Recall special recent memories • Record memories of the birth in a scrapbook or diary
• Difficult adjustment to a new daily routine	• Enjoy simple activities like a walk in the park, an ice cream cone, or playing on the floor with the baby • Take things one day at a time
Depression	• Seek guidance from your doctor for treating the physical causes • Be consistent with the therapy prescribed by the doctor to get through the most difficult phases • Set out to accomplish simple tasks each day
Other difficulties	
• With breastfeeding	• Strive to get regular naps and nighttime sleep • Get help with the feeding routine during emotionally difficult periods • Reduce caffeine, as it can increase anxiety and irritability • Consider discontinuing breastfeeding if it is contributing to physical or emotional difficulties • Eat a balanced diet, including fruits and vegetables • Drink at least eight glasses of liquid daily
• With getting back into shape	• Continue taking prenatal vitamins and iron • Establish some form of exercise program • Set a realistic plan (e.g., short walks around the block, swimming) • Be patient but diligent—do not expect overnight change

Appendix G

Goal-Setting in the Postpartum Period
(See Chapter Eight)

Week	Husband	Wife
1	Do the dinner dishes Take out the garbage	Shower by noon Start on baby announcements
2	Change diapers Take the family for a ride	Be dressed by noon Make the bed
3	Bathe the baby Go out for dinner together	Have makeup on by noon Dust
4	Make a meal Go grocery shopping	Do the laundry Take the baby for a walk
5	Take a walk together Vacuum	Make dinner Go on an outing

Week	Husband	Wife
1		
2		
3		
4		
5		
6		
7		
8		

Appendix H

Your Infant's Growth and Development
(See Chapter Nine)

First Month

Ability	Activities	Goal	Equipment
Lift head	• Allow the baby to lie on his stomach to play so that he will have to lift his head to see • Hold the baby upright against your shoulder	Strengthen and coordinate the baby's neck muscles	
Focus eyes	• Place colorful objects 1 to 3 feet away from the baby • When holding the baby, be close enough that he can make eye contact	Strengthen eye muscles	• Colorful mobiles • Black and white objects • A small mirror for the baby to see himself • Medium-sized colorful toys at eye level
Suck	• Routine nursing or bottle-feeding • Use of pacifier between feedings • The baby may suck on his hands or fingers	Develop lip, tongue, and cheek muscles for eating and speaking	• Orthodontically correct pacifier • Good quality nipples on bottles

One to Three Months

Ability	Activities	Goal	Equipment
Notice hands and feet	• Baby will play with his hands while lying on his tummy • Start hand and finger play songs, moving baby's hands for him • Baby will notice his feet when he is sitting in an infant seat or lying on the floor with his feet pulled up	Develop hand-eye coordination and body awareness	• Wrist rattles, shoes with bells, colorful socks • An infant seat will allow him to see his feet and legs

Ability	Activities	Goal	Equipment
Recognize sounds	• Talk to the baby as you give him care • Tell him short stories • Acknowledge him when you enter or leave the room	Distinguish among sounds and early language development	• Rattles • Radio
Vocalize (cooing)	Imitate baby's noise in response	Develop language skills	
Turn from stomach to back	• Place baby on his stomach with objects on either side to encourage him to reach for them • Play rolling games • Sit on the floor with the baby and gently rock him back and forth on his sides	Develop back, abdominal, leg, and arm muscles	

Three to Six Months

Ability	Activities	Goal	Equipment
• Reach for objects • Pass objects from hand to hand	• Have brightly colored objects within baby's reach • Hand objects to the baby to encourage him to grasp them • Attach toys to baby's car seat	• Develop hand-eye coordination • Develop hand muscles	• Toys that are small enough for the baby to hold, but too large for him to swallow • Rattles, balls, blocks, small stuffed animals, swing
Sit, first with support, and then alone	• Carry the baby in an upright position • Support him on your lap for playtime • Prop him into a sitting position with pillows when he is in his playpen or crib	Develop abdominal and back muscle strength and coordination	Walker, stroller (in a semi-reclining position until the baby is able to support himself in a sitting position)

Ability	Activities	Goal	Equipment
Show interest in body parts	• Sit the baby in front of a mirror and allow him to touch the baby in the mirror • Identify features on the baby's face, as well as on the faces of others • Do the same using pictures, dolls, stuffed animals	Develop identity	Mirrors, pictures, books, dolls, stuffed animals

Six to Nine Months

Ability	Activities	Goal	Equipment
Play Peek-a-Boo	• Play Peek-a-Boo • Play hide-and-seek with toys	Develop realization of the existence of objects that are not visible	
• Increase fine motor skills of the hands • Thumb and finger (pincher) grasp • Clap hands together	• Play finger games (Itsy-Bitsy Spider, This Little Piggy, Pat-a-Cake) • Offer small pieces of food (round, O-shaped cereal) that requires the baby to use his thumb and fingers to grasp		Small hand-sized toys
Show interest in feeding skills	• Allow the baby to hold his own spoon (experiment with pudding and cereal) and hold his own cup • Allow the baby to feed himself small crackers, a cut-up banana, etc.	• Feed self • Develop independence	• Small-handled spoon and fork (with blunt tines) • Sipper cup with handles
Crawl	• Allow him to spend time on the floor with ample space for movement • Encourage him to crawl to familiar toys or people	• Develop left- and right-brain coordination • Strengthen muscles	

Nine to Twelve Months

Ability	Activities	Goal	Equipment
Pull himself up to stand	• Place toys on a low table or chair seat at which the baby can easily stand to play • Stand the baby up by using both his hands	• Build self-confidence • Develop balance	• Toys • Steady chairs and tables
Walk	• Give him large rolling toys that he can push while walking • Hold his hand and encourage him to walk alongside you	• Build self-confidence • Develop balance and coordination	• Toy stroller or shopping cart • Combination pushing/sitting toy
Put objects into containers	• Allow him to play in a sandbox • At clean-up time, encourage him to put small toys in a container	Develop hand-eye coordination and fine motor skills	• Buckets with hand-sized balls or blocks • Small purse or backpack to hold favorite toys • Toy box

Glossary

Abruptio Placenta
The condition in which the placenta prematurely separates from the uterus.

Amniotic Fluid
The fluid that surrounds the baby within the uterus.

Amniotic Sac (bag of waters)
The sac surrounding the baby in the uterus. It contains the baby, the amniotic fluid, and the placenta.

Apgar Score
A rating system used to assess a baby at one and five minutes after birth.

Areola
The dark ring of tissue surrounding the nipple of the breast.

Blighted Ovum
A condition where there is no identifiable fetus in the amniotic sac.

Braxton-Hicks Contractions
Intermittent uterine contractions; usually do not cause discomfort and may become more pronounced in the later months of pregnancy.

Breech Baby
Baby born feet or bottom first instead of headfirst.

Cephalopelvic Disproportion (CPD)
The condition in which the baby's head is too large to pass through the mother's pelvis.

Cervix
The necklike opening of the uterus that dilates and effaces during labor to allow passage of the baby into the birth canal.

Cesarean Section
A surgery in which an incision is made through the abdomin and into the uterus to deliver the baby.

Circumcision
The surgical removal of the foreskin of the penis.

Colic
Spasms of the intestine accompanied by abdominal pain occurring in infants in the first few months.

Colostrum
A premilk, thick, yellow-colored fluid concentrated in calories. Produced in small amounts, it contains highly concentrated proteins and antibodies that are passed to the baby from the mother. Colostrum helps to prepare the baby's digestive tract for the absorption of food.

Contraction
The shortening and thickening of the uterus (a muscle) that is associated with labor pains.

Croup
An illness common in young children characterized by difficult, noisy breathing and loss of voice and accompanied by moderate fever.

Crowning

The appearance of the top of the baby's head at the vaginal opening.

Dilation

The gradual opening of the cervix during labor. Ten centimeters is considered fully dilated.

Duration

The time period measured from the beginning of a contraction to the end of that same contraction.

Effacement

The thinning and shortening of the cervix during labor. Measured in percentages. One hundred percent is considered fully effaced.

Effleurage

Light massage of the abdomen in labor. Usually performed by the mother using circular motions on the abdomen for comfort during contractions.

Engaged

Indicates that the presenting part of the baby has settled into the mother's pelvis.

Episiotomy

Surgical incision in the perineum to enlarge the vaginal opening.

Forceps

Instruments resembling salad tongs that are used to facilitate the movement of the head through the birth canal when delivery time must be shortened due to fetal distress or maternal exhaustion.

Frequency of Contraction
The period measured from the beginning of a contraction to the beginning of the next contraction.

Fundus
The upper, rounded portion of the uterus.

Hives
Eruption of tiny, itchy, red bumps on the skin caused by an allergic reaction to food or other substance.

Hyperventilation
Improper balance of carbon dioxide and oxygen in the blood due to accelerated breathing.

IM
An intramuscular injection.

Intensity
The strength of the uterine contractions.

IV
An intravenous line.

Jaundice
The yellow discoloration of the skin, whites of the eyes, and the mucous membranes from an increased concentration of bilirubin in the blood.

Kegel Exercise
Used to strengthen the pelvic floor muscles.

Lanugo

The fine hair that may be present on the baby's body after birth. Usually seen on the shoulders, forehead, cheeks, and back. Disappears within the first few weeks of life.

Lochia

The discharge of blood, mucus, and tissue from the uterus after the delivery of the baby.

Meconium

A dark green or black tarlike substance that is the baby's first bowel movement.

Membranes

The soft sheets of tissue that make up the sac (bag of waters) that encloses the baby in the uterus.

Morning Sickness

A basic condition and feeling of nausea that accompanies the first three months of pregnancy. This usually occurs in the morning but not always. To help minimize nausea, try eating a few soda crackers or dry toast right after getting up in the morning. Call your health care provider is morning sickness does not improve or you begin to experience prolong dehydration.

Multipara

A woman who has delivered more than one baby.

Oxytocin

A natural hormone that causes contractions of the uterus; also can be a synthetic replica of this hormone.

Perineum
The area between the vaginal opening and the rectum.

Placenta Previa
The condition in which the placenta partially or completely covers the cervical opening.

Placenta
The circular, flat organ in the pregnant uterus that serves as the exchange station for oxygen, nourishment, and the elimination of wastes (also known as the afterbirth.)

Placental Abruption
See abruptio placenta.

Posterior Position
The back of the baby's head is against the woman's spine during labor.

Postpartum
The six-week period following birth.

Presenting Part
The part of the baby that is closest to the cervical opening.

Primigravida
A woman giving birth to her first child.

Prolapsed Umbilical Cord
The umbilical cord slips below the presenting part of the baby, possibly cutting off his supply of oxygen if it is compressed.

PURE
Position, Urination, Relaxation, and Environment—tools to provide comfort to the laboring woman.

Show

The blood-tinged mucus discharge
from the vagina before and during labor.

Station

The position of the baby in relation to the
woman's pelvic bones (see figure G.1).

Figure G.1

Stretch Marks (striae)

Areas of the mother's skin that are stretched during pregnancy,
usually on the abdomen, breasts, legs, and buttocks.

Toxemia

A maternal condition characterized by high blood pressure, swelling
of the hands and face, and protein in the urine. If not treated, it may
lead to seizures.

Tucks

Compresses available in most drug stores, to be used in postpartum
care by mother.

Umbilical Cord

The cord that connects the baby to the placenta.

Uterus

A pear-shaped muscular organ that contains the membranes, amniotic fluid, and the baby during pregnancy.

Vacuum Extractor

A cone-shaped suction cup that is placed on the baby's head.
During the pushing stage, this suction helps to deliver the baby
by maintaining station between contractions.

Vagina

The canal leading from the uterus to outside the woman's body.

Vernix Caseosa

A white, cheeselike protective material covering the baby's skin at birth.

Notes

1. Bruce Wilkinson, *The Seven Laws of the Learner*, audiotape series. Published by Multnomah Press, Sisters, OR: 1992.

2. For a concise timeline of important changes in birth practices, see Appendix A, "A Timeline of Birth Practices."

3. We list these methods for the purpose of information and education, not necessarily for endorsement.

4. The collection of semen for analysis may be awkward for a couple undergoing treatment for infertility. The use of a sterile condom for semen collection may alleviate some of the dilemmas associated with the need to spontaneously produce a specimen. By using a sterile condom, a couple can produce a specimen through the normal act of marital intimacy, eliminating the need for the husband to produce the specimen on his own in a clinical setting. The couple should ask their infertility specialist about obtaining sterile condoms.

5. For ease of reading, we will refer to the primary health-care provider as a doctor or obstetrician and use masculine pronouns to refer to both doctors and babies (except in cases where the baby referred to is specified as female).

6. We encourage expectant parents to become proficient in infant CPR through classes offered by the American Red Cross or the American Heart Association.

7. Many doctors and hospitals no longer perform VBACs. If you have had a C-section previously and are considering a VBAC, be sure to talk with your doctor about it early in your pregnancy, as it may affect where you can deliver. Approximately 60 to 80 percent of women who attempt a VBAC deliver vaginally. Those with the best chance of doing so are women who previously had a bikini-cut incision, who have no major medical problems, and whose baby is normal size and is in a head-down position. The chance of success decreases if the reason for the first C-section is repeated in the subsequent pregnancy.

8. Parent-directed feeding is a philosophy for feeding your baby that is presented in the book, *"On Becoming Babywise"*.

9. Caleb Ministries is dedicated to helping parents through the loss of a child, as well as with infertility and the emotional after affects of abortion. For more information, write them at P.O. Box 470093, Charlotte, NC 28247, or call 1-877-4U-CALEB or 704-846-5372.

10. You can purchase or rent an electric pump. Check with your local hospital or pharmacy for availability. The following companies may offer nationwide service: Medella (1-800-435-8316) and Hollister (1-800-323-8750).

11. For more information, contact Lact-Aid International's hotline at 615-744-9090.

12. One such agency is Bethany Christian Services. With branch offices in many states, its mission is to place adoptive children in Christian homes.

Index